THE Passion CODE

100 Days with Jesus

O. S. Hawkins

D1304929

Published in Nashville, Tennessee, by Thomas Nelson. Thomas Nelson is a registered trademark of HarperCollins Christian Publishing, Inc.

Thomas Nelson titles may be purchased in bulk for educational, business, fund-raising, or sales promotional use. For information, please e-mail SpecialMarkets@ThomasNelson.com.

ISBN-13: 978-1-4002-1150-0 (hard cover)
ISBN-13: 978-1-4041-1583-5 (custom)

Printed in the United States of America

21 22 23 24 25 LSC 6 5 4 3 2 1

THE Passion CODE

100 Days with Jesus

O. S. Hawkins

COUNTRYMAN®
An Imprint of Thomas Nelson Publishers

THOMAS NELSON
Since 1798

TABLE OF CONTENTS

INTRODUCTION

The word *passion* can be defined as an intense desire. We use the word in the traffic patterns of life with such phrases as "He has a passion for golf" or "She has a passion for music." Our Lord Jesus was moved and motivated by a passion, an intense desire, to do His Father's will. This passion is consistently revealed throughout the New Testament. At a well in Samaria, He stated, "My food is to do the will of Him who sent Me, and to finish His work" (John 4:34). In Gethsemane's garden we hear Him pleading, "Father, if it is Your will, take this cup away from Me; nevertheless not My will, but Yours, be done" (Luke 22:42). This passion to do His Father's will led Him to the cross, where it became for Christ the passion of His suffering.

The Passion Code was written to move and motivate us to an intense desire to know and love Christ, to do His will. It takes us on a one-hundred-day journey with Jesus to discover the truth of Colossians 1:27: "To them God willed to make known what are the riches of the glory of this mystery among the Gentiles: which is Christ in you, the hope of glory." The *Code* is revealed at Bethlehem, where we find God *with* us. It continues to Golgotha, where we find God *for* us. And it culminates at Pentecost with the discovery that

God is not only with us and for us but can also come to take up residency in our lives—God *in* us.

Each daily reading embodies a Code Word that unlocks the truth of the devotional thought and serves as a daily reminder of that truth. Write it down. Keep it with you. Think about it throughout your day as it stirs you to apply truth to your daily life so that, as James says, you will become a "doer of the word and not a hearer only" (James 1:22). Each day also includes a Passion Proclamation—a Bible verse to apply to your life—as well as a prayer. Keep this prayer in your heart and pray it repeatedly throughout your day.

We have a God who still speaks to us today with His Word and through His Spirit. Ask God to begin to give you a passion, an intense desire, to know Him. For to know Him is to know life . . . abundant and eternal. Turn the page and begin your own journey of unlocking the blessings of God's Word through *The Passion Code*.

PART 1

GOD WITH US

"They shall call His name Immanuel . . . God with us."

—MATTHEW 1:23

Too often we only associate the incarnation with the Christmas season. But living with this truth that God Himself stepped out of heaven, clothed Himself in human flesh, and came to be "with us" should not simply be a seasonal discipline; rather, it should be a continuous, year-round reality. The Lord could never be "in us," much less die "for us," if He had not first come to be "with us."

There is no one like you. You are unique. No one has a fingerprint like yours, a DNA that exactly matches yours. Roots are important, and not just to plants. Your DNA shows what proclivities you may have regarding disease, intellect, temperament, and so much more.

There are forty-seven names listed in Matthew 1, most unpronounceable. Some are great, some not so great. From paupers to princes, shepherds to slaves, kings to harlots, spanning twenty-one centuries of human experience, the list ends in a stable on a starlit night with one name that is above every other name: Jesus!

The family tree of our Lord does not end with His ancestors, because His descendants—you and I—have been born again into His forever family.

Code Word: ROOTS

Can you tell me the full name of your great-grandfather? Or anything about his life? Chances are your own children's grandchildren will not even know *your* name. What really matters is this: are your true roots in Jesus' family tree?

Passion Proclamation

The book of the genealogy of Jesus Christ. . . . And Jacob begot Joseph the husband of Mary, of whom was born Jesus who is called Christ.

—MATTHEW 1:1, 16

Lord, may the roots of my life be sunk deep in Your truths, and may my passion for knowing You grow greater each day. In Jesus' name, amen.

T alk about heartbreak, sorrow, misery, and grief—all those things are woven through the fabric of our Lord's family tree. Can you feel their grief behind the words? The grief of Abraham leaving all he had known to go to a land where he had never been. The grief of letting go of his firstborn, Ishmael, whom he loved. And what about King David? He had a son who died in infancy because of David's own sin. Later, his son Absalom killed his brother Amnon, and if that were not enough to break a father's heart, Absalom led a revolt against his own dad.

But all these names in Christ's family tree don't hold a candle to the grief that many of us feel. Jesus understands the grief in His ancestors and His descendants. Perhaps your own heart is heavy. Perhaps you have been misunderstood. Jesus was. He says, "I understand." Perhaps you are lonely. Jesus says, "I know the loneliness of Gethsemane's garden." He will bear your griefs and carry your sorrows . . . if you will let Him.

CODE WORD: GRIEF

Jesus understands your grief. Behind the lives of all these men and women in His family tree, we see grief, but they made it . . . and so can you.

Passion Proclamation

Abraham begot Isaac. . . . David the king begot Solomon by her who had been the wife of Uriah.

—MATTHEW 1:2, 6

Lord, thank You for bearing my grief and carrying my sorrows. I am leaning on You. In Jesus' name, amen.

DAY 3

If time permitted, we could stop at each of the dozens of names in Christ's genealogy and speak of the grace behind their lives. But there are four obvious testimonies of grace that should catch our eyes. They are all women, and in that ancient world it was unheard-of to see women listed in genealogy tables.

First is Tamar (Matthew 1:3). Who was she? Let me introduce her. She once dressed as a prostitute, seduced her father-in-law, and had an illegitimate child (Genesis 38). We also read of Rahab (Matthew 1:5). She was the town prostitute of ancient Jericho. Next comes Ruth (v. 5). She was a member of a race that began in incest and worshiped pagan gods. Finally we meet Bathsheba (v. 6). She lived in adultery with King David.

How did these women find their way into Jesus' own family tree? Only one word: *grace!* God's unmerited favor.

CODE WORD: FAVOR

There is good news: where sin abounds, grace much more abounds (see Romans 5:20). What is the Lord telling us? I don't think He was speaking softly when He declared, "If anyone is in Christ, he is a new creation; old things have passed away; behold, all things have become new" (2 Corinthians 5:17).

Passion Proclamation

Salmon begot Boaz by Rahab, Boaz begot Obed by Ruth.
—MATTHEW 1:5

Lord, thank You for giving me what I never deserved . . . an amazing gift: grace! In Jesus' name, amen.

Note carefully what today's verse says . . . and doesn't say. It does not say, "Joseph begot Jesus." Here the repetition of the "begots" ends. The "whom" in Greek is feminine singular, referring only to Mary and not to Joseph. Can you see God the Father right here in the family tree of Jesus? Jesus was the virgin-born son of Mary, in whose womb the Father implanted His Son. Hundreds of years earlier, the prophet Isaiah had said the virgin birth would be the "sign" of the long-awaited Messiah (Isaiah 7:14).

It is because Jesus was Mary's seed (the seed of a woman, Genesis 3:15) and not the seed of Joseph that entitles Him to be your Savior and Lord. The virgin birth is the bedrock of His authority.

Some see only grief. But look closer and you will find grace. And if you look close enough, you will see the hand of God molding, making, forming, and fashioning you. He has been there all along.

CODE WORD: BOOK

The only book that ultimately matters is the Lamb's Book of Life, where the names of all those who have put their trust in Christ are listed. Is your name in that book? Jesus said, "Do not rejoice . . . that the spirits are subject to you, but rather rejoice because your names are written in heaven" (Luke 10:20).

Passion Proclamation

And Jacob begot Joseph the husband of Mary, of whom was born Jesus who is called Christ.

—MATTHEW 1:16

Lord, thank You that You are working in my life this very moment, forming and fashioning me into Your very image. In Jesus' name, amen.

DAY 5

If you are like me, you type hundreds of words each day. Let me ask you a question: Are the keys you type on black, gray, or white? The truth is, most people cannot give a definitive answer without looking at the keys, even though they look at them several times every single day. The point? There are a lot of things in life we see but don't really see.

Take the nativity scene. You have seen it depicted thousands of times, but have you really *seen* it? I love the feature on my mobile phone that allows me to crop my photos. Recently we took a family picture. Susie and I are in the middle, with the grandkids and their parents flanking us. We have a common "enemy" with our grandkids—their parents! I cropped them out and have a beautiful photo of Susie, me, and the grandkids!

Let's crop the nativity. Look at the entire nativity scene. It is a worship service. Crop it a bit and you find a family in the middle: Joseph, Mary, and the Christ. Crop it more and in the center you see Jesus only.

Code Word: CROP

Can you see the nativity scene in your mind? Crop out everything but Jesus. He, and He alone, is the center of everything. Keep Him in the very center of your life today.

PASSION PROCLAMATION

She brought forth her firstborn Son . . . and laid Him in a manger.

—LUKE 2:7

Lord, with all that is swarming around me today, help me focus on You. In Jesus' name, amen.

DAY 6

Look at the nativity, and you see a worship service. Angels hover over it like drones. Common, smelly shepherds and sophisticated wise men bow down. Worship flows from everyone toward the child.

It is difficult to imagine any greater contrasts than what we see at the nativity. They were different socially. Shepherds were low on the socioeconomic scale. Wise men were so socially acceptable they entered the king's palace. They were different educationally. Shepherds had no formal education, while the wise men were famed for knowledge. God is telling us that no matter who we are or where we are from, any and all can come to Christ and worship Him.

All of life, first and foremost, is about worship. Those at the manger were not there simply admiring this child. They were worshiping Him. Make sure worship is a priority each and every day.

CODE WORD: ALL

Think about it: lowly shepherds and elite wise men all huddled together in worship. Because Jesus didn't come for only the elite or even only the lowly. He came for all—any and all who will join these gathered around the manger to bow before Him.

Passion Proclamation

Glory to God in the highest, and on earth peace, goodwill toward men!

—LUKE 2:14

Lord, help me keep the worship of You first in my heart. Glory to God in the highest. In Jesus' name, amen.

DAY 7

Look in the middle of the nativity and you find a little family. God entrusted His own Son to a human family, just like yours. He could have circumvented the family, but He didn't. God put His own stamp of approval on the family.

Family is important to God. Think about it. He instituted the family long before He did the church. He placed His own Son in a family with relationships and domestic responsibilities. So Jesus was raised in Nazareth in a family unit.

Later, while hanging on the cross, He spotted Mary and instructed John to care for her. Jesus was a family man. His was a blended family, when you think about it. Family is precious to Him.

The nativity has a family in the middle of it for good reason. God is pro-family. Jesus has His own unique way of drawing families together.

Code Word: FAMILY

Where do we most want to be when we're traveling for days on end? Home. We drive long distances to sleep on couches and floors to be at our family's home for visits. Make sure you hold your family close to your heart, and don't be hesitant to say, "I love you."

Passion Proclamation

So it was, that while they were there, the days were completed for her to be delivered.

—LUKE 2:6

Lord, thank You for family, and help me do my part in drawing my family closer to each other and to You. In Jesus' name, amen.

DAY 8

I love Rembrandt's portrayal of the nativity. One great beam of light falls upon the baby Jesus so that all the other participants are somewhat shrouded in shadow. He wanted nothing to take away from the significance of Christ.

All of life should center on Christ. And primarily, Christ alone. Not only is He the center of the nativity scene; He is the center of all of human history. His birth divided all of human history into "before" and "after" Christ. And if you don't believe this, just think about it at the end of the year when you change your calendar. His birth points the way for all men and women to see that the road to our eternal home is through Him.

If the nativity were your own life, who or what would be in the center? Jesus longs to be the center of your life.

CODE WORD: TRANSPORT

If you could transport yourself back in time to that stable, would you see yourself standing somewhere off to the side, observing? Or would you find yourself on your knees, joining the angelic choir and singing, "Glory to God in the highest" (Luke 2:14)?

Passion Proclamation

There is born to you this day in the city of David a Savior, who is Christ the Lord.

—LUKE 2:11

Lord, my desire is to be a worshiper. And You alone are worthy of my worship. In Jesus' name, amen.

DAY 9

It was a dark night . . . yet there was light! The Light of the world had come. Bethlehem almost missed it. No room. So the young, pregnant Jewish girl found herself without the decency of even a clean sheet or a simple cot. In her hour of labor, her bed was straw in a stable. And when the Babe was born, she herself, with trembling fingers, wrapped Him in cloths and laid Him in the feeding trough.

Down the hillside a group of shepherds had a surprise visit from heaven. They rushed to the stable, found the Babe, and returned "glorifying and praising God" (Luke 2:20).

Let's become Bethlehem ourselves. We find in this little village a place of potential, providence, and privilege. The Lord longs for you to become a Bethlehem in your own right. That is, to awaken to the fact that you are a person of potential, providence, and privilege.

CODE WORD: SURPRISE

Can you imagine the surprise of the shepherds that night when heaven burst open before them and the angelic chorus in perfect harmony declared the Lord's birth? This is usually the way it happens . . . surprised by God. Be prepared for Him to meet you in surprising ways.

Passion Proclamation

Let us now go to Bethlehem and see this thing that has come to pass, which the Lord has made known to us.

—LUKE 2:15

Lord, help me live in anticipation of a heavenly surprise this day. In Jesus' name, amen.

Think of it. Of all the places for the Messiah to be born, God chose Bethlehem. One would have thought it might be in a much more prominent place, like Jerusalem. Bethlehem reminds us that in God's economy the small shall become great, and the last shall be first. Bethlehem was a place of potential, and even though you may feel insignificant, like Bethlehem, so are you!

As the Lord looks at you, He doesn't see you for what you are, but for what you could become. This is the message of Bethlehem. God did not come to Caesar's palace to be born, nor to Herod's court. He arrived quietly, almost unannounced in a seemingly insignificant village.

God is reminding you today that in His eyes you have potential for greatness. See yourself as a Bethlehem. You, too, are a person of potential.

CODE WORD: PROSPECT

Your prospects are limitless. God sees you not for who you are, but for who you can become. When He first saw Peter, He said, "You are a small pebble but will become a great rock" (John 1:42, author's paraphrase). Peter believed it and later became the leader of the early church.

Passion Proclamation

"But you, Bethlehem . . . though you are little among the thousands of Judah, yet out of you shall come forth . . . the One . . . whose goings forth are from of old, from everlasting."

—MICAH 5:2

Lord, help me see today what You see—incredible potential in me. In Jesus' name, amen.

DAY 11

Long centuries before His birth, the prophets foretold that Christ would be born in Bethlehem. But how? Joseph and Mary resided seventy miles north, in Nazareth. God put the whole world in motion to fulfill His Word. A decree went out from Caesar Augustus that everyone was to go to the place of their family lineage to pay taxes. So Joseph, because he was of the line of David, left Nazareth with his very pregnant wife on a long journey of inconvenience.

Many of the things in our lives that on the surface appear inconvenient may just be the hand of God's providence getting us to our own Bethlehem.

Bethlehem reminds us that what God promises, He performs—no matter what. Bethlehem is a place of providence, and so are you.

CODE WORD: PROVIDENCE

God is at work, behind the scenes in your life, right now: "The Most High rules in the kingdom of men" (Daniel 4:17). God has not abdicated His throne. He is at work in your life when you are not even aware.

Passion Proclamation

For the eyes of the LORD run to and fro throughout the whole earth, to show Himself strong on behalf of those whose heart is loyal to Him.

—2 CHRONICLES 16:9

Lord, what You have promised You will perform. Make me a Bethlehem today. In Jesus' name, amen.

DAY 12

What an awesome privilege to be the handpicked city to cradle the Son of God. Why Bethlehem? Why not Jerusalem, the seat of religious power? Or Rome, the center of political power? Or Athens, the center of intellectual power? God was sending a message. The hope of our world is not in religion, politics, or philosophy. God privileged the little village of Bethlehem to send the message—the hope of the world is in a Savior!

This day could become a Bethlehem moment for you. Like Bethlehem, you can awaken to a brand-new world. The same Christ born in Bethlehem can be born again in you. Paul put it this way: "I labor in birth again until Christ is formed in you." If you think Bethlehem is privileged to be His birthplace, what a greater privilege for Christ to be born in you.

CODE WORD: EXPECTATION

Hope is the sense of expectation that something good is going to happen. Bethlehem almost missed the moment. But you can awaken to a brand-new hope by allowing your life to become a Bethlehem—with the great privilege of having Christ born again in you.

Passion Proclamation

My little children, for whom I labor in birth again until Christ is formed in you . . .

—GALATIANS 4:19

Lord, thank You, not just for hope but for the realization that You are truly alive in me, in this moment. In Jesus' name, amen.

DAY 13

There is an interesting psychology in the naming of our children. Some are named with family names to retain a family heritage. I am often asked what *O. S.* stands for, and I am quick to say, "Omar Sharif." But the truth is, my initials represent family names—Otis Swafford. And now you know why I used O. S. on the cover of this book. Others are named for an attribute their parents desire their child to achieve in life: Faith or Hope, for example.

In the Bible, names have specific meanings. Jesus changed Simon's name to Peter because He saw the potential for him to be a "rock." Joseph's name was changed to Barnabas (which means "Son of Encouragement") because every time he had center stage, he was encouraging the early believers.

During these days let's pause to think of the names given to our Lord. The very mission of Christ is in His name: Jesus. And the message of Christ is in His name as well: Immanuel—God with us!

Code Word: NAME

What does your name mean? The next time you sign a check or a note and look at your name, think about it. Names matter . . . and the one name that is above all others is *Jesus*!

Passion Proclamation

Therefore God also has highly exalted Him and given Him the name which is above every name.

—PHILIPPIANS 2:9

Lord, help me wear the name "Christian" with integrity and honor today. In Jesus' name, amen.

DAY 14

The name *Jesus* is a transliteration of the Hebrew name *Joshua*, which means "Jehovah saves." His very name, Jesus, tells us of His mission when He came from heaven to earth—to "save His people from their sins."

Jesus is our Lord's intensely personal name. Have you noticed how difficult it is for some people to say this name, Jesus? They find it much easier to refer to Him as God or Lord or Christ or "the Man upstairs." But there is something about speaking the name Jesus. Say it now. Out loud. Jesus is His most personal name, and only those who truly know Him in the free pardoning of their sin find it easy to speak His name.

He came to save you from your sins. Open your heart to Him, for He said, "I came to seek and to save those who were lost" (Luke 19:10, author's paraphrase).

Code Word: LOST

Say that word: *lost*. Say it again out loud. Without Christ that is what we are—lost beyond hope, lost beyond time, lost beyond eternity, lost, forever lost. But when we open our hearts to Him, we begin to know Him by His up-close and personal name: Jesus!

Passion Proclamation

And she will bring forth a Son, and you shall call His name JESUS, for He will save His people from their sins.

—MATTHEW 1:21

Jesus, thank You for coming on a mission for the express purpose of saving me. In Jesus' name, amen.

The name *Immanuel* is a translation of two Hebrew words expressing "God is with us." *God* with us. Not some prophet or teacher or holy man. But God Himself clothed in human flesh—*with us*! He came to where we are so we could go eternally to where He is. God . . . always with us.

God—that is majesty. With us—that is mercy. God—that is glory. With us—that is grace. He came to be with us, to give us what we never deserved and to *not* give us what we did deserve.

He could not be Jesus without being Immanuel. That is, to save us, He first had to come and be with us, taking on human flesh. At Bethlehem we see God with us. At Calvary we see God for us. At Pentecost we see God in us.

CODE WORD: WITH

It is one thing to be *for* someone but another thing to be *with* someone, to stand by his or her side in good times as well as bad, times of sorrow as well as times of joy. This is our Lord's name: Immanuel. He is with you right now. And when He left this earth, He did so with these final words: "Lo, I am with you always" (Matthew 28:20).

Passion Proclamation

"And they shall call His name Immanuel," which is translated, "God with us."

—MATTHEW 1:23

Lord, nowhere I go today will I be without You. You are with me always. In Jesus' name, amen.

DAY 16

What is a sign? It is something that is intended to do two things: grab your attention and then tell you something. You may be driving on a hazardous mountain road and see a flashing sign warning you to slow down for a sharp curve ahead. Billboards are designed to grab your attention, to do it fast, and then to leave you with a message you won't soon forget.

The Bible tells us there is a "sign" regarding the promised coming Messiah. And this sign, designed to get our attention and tell us something, is that a "virgin shall conceive and bear a Son." This is humanly impossible. It would take a divine miracle.

Jesus was virgin-born. He was not God and man. He is the God-man, the "only begotten Son . . . of the Father" (John 1:18), who put His own seed in a young virgin girl.

CODE WORD: SIGN

Today, as you run your errands and see a hundred signs grabbing your attention to tell you something, let each one be a reminder that the "sign" that Jesus is Lord is the virgin birth, the bedrock of your salvation.

Passion Proclamation

The Lord Himself will give you a sign: Behold, the virgin shall conceive and bear a Son, and shall call His name Immanuel.

—ISAIAH 7:14

Lord, if I could understand it all, then there wouldn't be much to understand. I believe . . . by faith . . . even all that I don't understand. In Jesus' name, amen.

DAY 17

These words grab my heart more than any others: "She . . . laid Him in a manger" (Luke 2:7). Not a nice little wooden cradle like we see in a manger scene. But a rock-hewn cattle trough in a cave-like stable where your sandals squashed in the dung as you walked and the nauseating smell of the animals filled your nostrils. She laid Him in a manger. Think of it. Sickness, disease, death were likely possibilities.

How desperately alone from family and friends Mary must have felt when she realized the babe would be born far away from home. In her hour of pain, her bed was straw in a stable, and when the baby was born, she herself, with trembling fingers, "wrapped Him in swaddling cloths, and laid Him in a manger" (v. 7).

"No room" was not just the message of Bethlehem but the theme of Jesus' life. Yet it is those who find Him and make room in their hearts for Him who understand the true message of why He came.

Code Word: ACCESS

Had Jesus been born in a palace, like most kings, few could have reached Him without gaining permission. But no one, no matter how poor or how rich, has difficulty accessing a stable. What access is behind those beautiful and welcoming words, "She . . . laid Him in a manger."

Passion Proclamation

For "whoever calls on the name of the Lord shall be saved."
—ROMANS 10:13

Lord, thank You that anyone may come to You . . . and that includes me. In Jesus' name, amen.

DAY 18

Mary. A young girl playing in the streets of Nazareth with her friends one day, and finding she is pregnant, though a virgin and unmarried, the next. Her initial response? "How can this be?" (Luke 1:34).

After Jesus was born, it all began to sink in; Mary "pondered" all these things in her heart. The word picture is of a cake, with all the ingredients in a bowl, being stirred up. She was putting it all together, stirring it up in her mind . . . the prophecies . . . the angel's message . . . the virgin birth.

She knew those chubby little hands would never be adorned with expensive gold or silver rings. They were destined for other things, like touching lepers, forming clay out of spittle for blind eyes, and eventually being pierced with Roman spikes. But she also knew that millions of us would follow in His steps. She "pondered" all these things and kept them to herself.

CODE WORD: BAKE

If you are like me, you enjoy pastries. Let each bite remind you of Mary pondering all those things in her heart. Get by yourself, contemplate it, meditate on it, and ponder the wonder of Bethlehem.

Passion Proclamation

But Mary kept all these things and pondered them in her heart.

—LUKE 2:19

Lord, I honor You in pausing to give honor to the woman You chose to nurture Your own Son. Help me to be a ponderer this day and every day. In Jesus' name, amen.

DAY 19

Joseph is the one person in the story of Christ's birth who is seldom mentioned and never quoted, yet the entire narrative hinges on his faithfulness. Mary is quoted. As are Elizabeth, Zacharias, the shepherds, the wise men, Herod, Simeon, and even the angels. But there is no record of anything Joseph ever said.

We have hymns and songs about Mary, the wise men, the shepherds, the angels, even the star. But look in any hymnbook, and you will not find a song about Joseph.

There is a reason God chose Joseph to mentor and raise His own son. He was faithful. Each time God sent him a message through an angel, he obeyed immediately (Matthew 1:18–25; 2:13–15; 2:20–22). Our legacy from this forgotten man at the manger is not in what he said but in what he did. The entire story hinges on his obedience to God.

Code Word: ORDINARY

Maybe no one takes notes of what you say. Perhaps you have never written a book. Like me, you are just an ordinary person. Learn a lesson from another one of us regular folks: Joseph, a common carpenter. God uses ordinary people. He chooses people like you and me to do as He commands.

Passion Proclamation

An angel . . . appeared to him . . . saying, "Joseph, . . . do not be afraid to take to you Mary your wife, for that which is conceived in her is of the Holy Spirit."

—MATTHEW 1:20

Lord, help me see that what I do speaks louder than anything I might say. In Jesus' name, amen.

DAY 20

As you're reading this, it may be April or August. It may even be December. But whatever the date, resolve to make room for Christmas today. Because when Christmas does roll around at the end of every year, we get so caught up in the season—decorating the house and tree, getting that special gift, seeing relatives, and getting invited to that certain someone's party—but then the season ends, and we leave it all behind until next year. It shouldn't be that way.

Today—whether it's winter or the heat of summer—join the shepherds in "glorifying and praising God." Make this day a time of celebration. God "inhabitest the praises" of His people (Psalm 22:3 KJV). This is where and when God feels at home—in the midst of your praise. So welcome Him today.

And note this: the shepherds "returned." Where? To their homes and businesses, to their daily lives. What an impact this must have had on those who knew them best. May God give you the grace to follow these shepherds and make Christmas a part of every day of the year.

CODE WORD: JOY

Celebrate Christ above all other things. Sing it—"Joy to the world, the Lord has come!"

Passion Proclamation

Then the shepherds returned, glorifying and praising God for all the things that they had heard and seen, as it was told them.

—LUKE 2:20

Lord, thank You for the joy only You can give. Let's celebrate Your birth each and every day! In Jesus' name, amen.

DAY 21

The reality that God is "with us" should not simply be celebrated, but circulated. The shepherds became verbal witnesses of what they had seen and heard. They had seen God in human flesh. Their own eyes had looked upon the One the prophets had foretold for centuries. They heard the music of heaven. And they could not help but speak to others about what they had seen and heard.

God chose a bunch of simple shepherds to be the first to circulate the good news of Christ's coming. Others in Bethlehem were of more importance and higher prominence. Surely their testimony would have borne more weight. But God still has His ways of confounding the wise.

The incarnation is just another warm and fuzzy, sentimental story unless you circulate it. When our daughter Wendy was a child, we informed her about a big family trip in the making with a request to not tell anyone about it yet. Her response was profound: "Daddy, what good is good news if you can't share it?"

Code Word: TELL

Jesus tells us to "go and tell" (see Matthew 28:19–20). We seem to find it much easier and safer to change this to "come and hear." Ask God to give you the boldness of the shepherds to make "widely known" the true message of Jesus and why He came.

Passion Proclamation

Now when they had seen Him, they made widely known the saying which was told them concerning this Child.

—LUKE 2:17

Lord, I want to deliver Your good news. And the headline reads "Jesus saves." In Jesus' name, amen.

DAY 22

All over our world, theaters large and small are presenting plays and pageants. What amazes me is how much goes on backstage before the curtain ever rises. There are props to be made, costumes to be sewn, music to be rehearsed, lines to be memorized, and so much more.

At Jesus' birth, with all the attention on Bethlehem and the manger, think for a minute about what was transpiring backstage . . . in heaven, that is. Our Lord was saying a farewell to His Father. Laying aside His glory, He stepped over the portals of heaven into a smelly Eastern stable.

And what would He say to the Father as He departed, when the curtain rose on the greatest event in human history? "I go to do Your will."

That for which we had been waiting and to which the prophets had been pointing was coming . . . and for the express purpose of doing the Father's will.

CODE WORD: BACKSTAGE

All of heaven was looking over those portals that starlit night in Bethlehem. The "fulness of the time" had come (Galatians 4:4 KJV). Although most on earth were oblivious, those in heaven were watching and worshiping. Remember: what is onstage is not always the whole story.

Passion Proclamation

"I have come . . . to do Your will."

—HEBREWS 10:7

Lord, to think of what You left to come to give me life moves me to want "to do Your will." In Jesus' name, amen.

What a step—from the splendor of heaven to the womb of a woman and finally to a stable in Bethlehem. There is so much behind the words "a body You have prepared for Me." God is Spirit, and yet He stepped into a body of flesh to identify with you and, ultimately, to be your own sin bearer.

This is condescension of the first and finest order. God became as helpless as a tiny seed planted in the womb of a young virgin girl. Then as helpless as a baby totally dependent on someone else's care.

Look at Mary. To paraphrase the master wordsmith Max Lucado, "She is in labor . . . her back is aching . . . her feet are swollen . . . she is sweating profusely . . . and having rapid contractions. The baby's head appears as she groans and pushes Him into the world. And He arrives!" God in flesh has come to visit us: "a body You have prepared for Me."

CODE WORD: BODY

Pinch yourself. Flesh, that is what God became . . . for you. So that He might say, "I understand." He came down to take a physical body so that one day you could go up and have a spiritual body. He came to be with you so that you could one day go to be with Him.

Passion Proclamation

When He came into the world, He said: . . . "A body You have prepared for Me."

—HEBREWS 10:5

Lord, there is nothing I go through that You don't understand. In Jesus' name, amen.

J esus not only comprehended the Father's will; He came to perform it. This is the primary purpose of His advent, to do the Father's will. He commenced this theme at birth and concluded with it thirty-three years later in Gethsemane's garden: "Not My will, but Yours, be done" (Luke 22:42).

There are two very important one-syllable, two-letter words in our scripture for the day: "I have come . . . *to do* Your will." The Lord didn't come to find the will of the Father but "to do" His will. His journey to Golgotha was not primarily to save us, but to be obedient to His Father's will.

Should we do less? True success in your life comes not in knowing the will of God but in doing it.

CODE WORD: PEACE

Peace is one of the most beautiful attributes of Christ. And doing the Father's will is what brings true peace. No wonder we call Him the "Prince of Peace" (Isaiah 9:6).

PASSION PROCLAMATION

When He came into the world, He said: . . . "I have come . . . to do Your will."

—HEBREWS 10:5–7

Lord, as You guide me to do Your will, put Your peace on me, the peace You give that the world cannot take away. In Jesus' name, amen.

DAY 25

It's a Christological miracle: "The Word became flesh and dwelt among us" (John 1:14).

Jesus was the unique God-man. As God, He walked on water, calmed the storm, healed the sick, and rose from the dead. As man, He got thirsty and tired; He felt sorrow and pain.

Jesus came to earth as a helpless, tiny seed planted in the womb of a young Jewish virgin. Forty weeks later, Jesus was born in a filthy stable.

Jesus was born in Bethlehem. Its name meaning "the house of bread," Bethlehem was the birthplace of the Bread of Life. God wanted people to know that the hope of the world is a Savior.

In the midst of all the hustle and bustle that today may bring, pause a moment and join Paul in exclaiming, "Thanks be to God for His indescribable gift!" (2 Corinthians 9:15).

Code Word: LOVE

The very definition of our Lord is this: "God is love" (1 John 4:8). Love is the oxygen of the kingdom. Without it there is no Christianity. "For God so loved the world that He gave His only begotten Son" (John 3:16). Believe on Him.

Passion Proclamation

Thanks be to God for His indescribable gift!
— 2 CORINTHIANS 9:15

Lord, I love You because You first loved me. In Jesus'
name, amen.

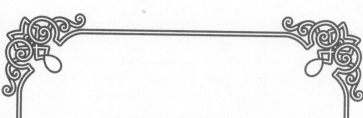

PART 2

GOD FOR US

While we were still sinners, Christ died for us.
—ROMANS 5:8

It is wonderful to know that God is "with us." But how much more so when we understand that He also came to be "for us." The journey that began in Bethlehem was for the single purpose of getting Christ to Golgotha, where He died "for us."

God proved His love toward us. He did not prove it by writing "I love you" in flaming letters across the sky. Instead, in "the fullness of the time . . . God sent forth His Son" (Galatians 4:4). Jesus was no remedial action or some kind of last-minute splint for a broken world when all else had failed. He came right on time, and He "demonstrate[d] His own love toward us, in that while we were still sinners, Christ died for us" (Romans 5:8).

The phenomenal aspect of His love is that it was expressed not when we were perfect or deserving. He loved us "while we were still sinners." Think of that! And that is not all. The ultimate proof of His love toward us is that He "died for us." The price He paid to prove His love was great. Every lash of the whip across His back, every *thud* of the hammer driving spikes in His hands and feet, was the voice of God saying, "I love sinners."

I remember when our first child was born, holding her in my arms and thinking, *I would give her the world if I could.* Then the thought occurred to me that God had said just the opposite: "I will give My only Son to the world." No wonder the songwriter of old said, "Oh, the love that drew salvation's plan! Oh, the grace that brought it down to man . . . at Calvary."[1]

Code Word: THUMB

Today, when you wash your hands, look at your thumb and let it remind you that no one has a thumbprint or DNA just like yours. You are an individual, indescribably loved by God. Let Him love you today.

Passion Proclamation

But when the fullness of the time had come, God sent forth His Son, born of a woman, born under the law.

—GALATIANS 4:4

Lord, if You love me even in those moments when I am so unlovely, help me love those around me as You have loved me. In Jesus' name, amen.

DAY 27

An unusual event transpires on Ash Wednesday each year. We often see men and women with ashes in the form of a cross on their foreheads. It is a visible reminder that "dust [we] are, and to dust [we] shall return" (Genesis 3:19). It begins for many a period of fasting and self-denial. But we should remember that the only way to please God is not by what we do—or refrain from doing—but by accepting His gracious offer of forgiveness made possible through Christ's shed blood on the cross.

Salvation is God's work, not our work. "For by grace you have been saved" (Ephesians 2:8a). Our salvation begins with Jesus—not with us. It is not His response to any good works we may do or evil works from which we've refrained. Salvation is provided for us wholly because of His grace, His unmerited favor toward you and me. The Father did not send His only Son to die for our sins because we kept begging and pleading for Him to do so. It was by His grace alone.

Salvation is God's work in God's way, not our way. It is "through faith . . . not of yourselves; it is the gift of God" (Ephesians 2:8b). I want to shout those words—"Through faith . . . not of yourselves . . . not of works!" No amount of doing good deeds or abstaining from certain pleasures can earn God's favor. Salvation is wholly by grace, through our faith in Christ alone . . . God's gift to us.

Code Word: DONE

No matter what you do or don't do, or what you give or give up, your salvation is not spelled D-O but D-O-N-E! Today remember that Christ paid a huge price to redeem you. It is already done! Your part is to receive this gift by faith.

Passion Proclamation

[It is] not by works of righteousness which we have done, but according to His mercy He saved us.

—TITUS 3:5

Lord, thank You for giving me what I never deserved—grace! And for Your mercy in not giving me what I do deserve. No wonder we call it "amazing grace"! In Jesus' name, amen.

*R*epentance has become one of the forgotten words in our English vocabulary. Yet it was the message of all the prophets. It was the message John the Baptist preached in the Jordan Valley. It was the message of Jesus as He commenced His ministry, saying, "Repent, for the kingdom of heaven is at hand" (Matthew 4:17). It was the message that birthed the church at Pentecost and the message of all the apostles.

But what really is behind this word? Repentance is not remorse, being sorry for our sin. The rich young ruler went away "sorrowful" but didn't repent (Matthew 19:16–22). It is not simply regret, wishing that some moment could be lived over again. Pilate washed his hands, regretting his evil deed, but he didn't repent (Matthew 27:24). Repentance is not reform, that is, trying to turn over a new leaf. Judas reformed by returning the silver coins of betrayal but didn't repent (Matthew 27:3).

Repentance emerges from a Greek word meaning "to change one's mind," which results in a change of will, which in turn results in a change of action. While repentance begins with a change of mind, the real proof will be found in a change of attitude and action.

CODE WORD: CHANGE

Begin today to change your mind about your *sin*. It is not some vice to be laughed off. Sin is so serious it necessitated the cross. Also change your mind about your *self*. You cannot please God through self-righteousness. Finally, change your mind about your *Savior*. Jesus is not just some teacher or prophet, but He is God, who clothed Himself in human flesh and gave Himself for you.

Passion Proclamation

Repent . . . , that your sins may be blotted out, so that times of refreshing may come from the presence of the Lord.

—ACTS 3:19

Lord, I can't excuse my sin by claiming everyone else is doing it, nor can I minimize it by asserting it is not as bad as someone else's. I confess: I have sinned against You, and I am wholly dependent on Your grace and mercy. In Jesus' name, amen.

DAY 29

The essence of biblical repentance is embedded beautifully in the old and often-repeated story of the prodigal son. The young man found himself not only broke—having left his family home and spent his inheritance—but broken. While feeding swine in a pigpen, he actually longed for the husks they were eating, and he "came to himself" (Luke 15:17). This first step in the repentance process, this change of mind, brought about the second step, a change in his will, his volition. In the next verse he exclaimed, "I will arise and go to my father." Once his mind and will were changed, his actions were sure to follow. Thus we read, "He arose and came to his father" (v. 20).

Repentance is a change of mind. That is it! And how do we know that we have truly changed our minds? Our volition will be changed as well, and our changed actions—resulting in a new life direction—will follow as naturally as water running downhill.

Repentance and faith are inseparable, born at the same time. They are two sides of the same coin. Repentance alone will not get you to heaven, but you can't get there without it. No wonder Jesus said, "Repent, for the kingdom of heaven is at hand" (Matthew 4:17).

Code Word: PROBE

Ask God today to bring to the surface of your heart and mind that thing that displeases Him and for which you need to repent. Then change your mind about it, and your will and actions will follow.

Passion Proclamation

Search me, O God, and know my heart. . . . See if there is any wicked way in me, and lead me in the way everlasting.
—PSALM 139:23–24

Lord, I am willing; I am willing to be made willing! Grant to me repentance and faith today. I throw myself upon Your mercy and stand in Your grace. In Jesus' name, amen.

I love the way the apostle Paul framed the subject of repentance: "The goodness of God leads you to repentance" (Romans 2:4). Once, when our daughters were small, my wife and I rented a vacation home deep in the Smoky Mountains. That first night in that strange place was, as author and educator James Weldon Johnson put it, "blacker than a hundred midnights down in a cypress swamp"![2]

I was awakened in the middle of the night by the cries of our little seven-year-old at the top of the stairs. I bounded up the stairs to find her disoriented and scared in the darkness. I took her by the hand and led her down the stairs into the security of our own bed, where she soundly slept the rest of the night away.

And so it is that our dear Lord finds us in the night, often disoriented by the issues of life. He takes us by the hand, and, as the Bible says, His own goodness "leads [us] to repentance."

When all is said and done, what difference will it make if we drive luxury cars, eat vitamin-enriched foods, live in palatial homes, and are buried in mahogany caskets if we rise up in judgment to meet a God we do not know? Let His goodness take you by the hand today. He will lead you to repentance.

Code Word: HAND

It may be that for too long you have called all the shots. Put your hand in His hand today. Go ahead; do it. He will lead you to repentance.

Passion Proclamation

The goodness of God leads you to repentance.

—ROMANS 2:4

Lord, I am amazed at Your love for me. You are a good God, and I put my hand in Yours today. Lead me in the way I should go. In Jesus' name, amen.

DAY 31

The Bible says, "And the Word became flesh and dwelt among us" (John 1:14). Who is this "Word"? It is God Himself, stepping out of heaven, clothing Himself in human flesh, and physically invading human history. John leaves no doubt concerning this identity: "In the beginning was the Word, and the Word was with God, and *the Word was God*" (John 1:1).

Jesus came down to where we are so that we could one day go to where He is! He came not clinging to the brightness of His glory, not shunning us for our sinful condition, but humbling Himself and taking on a garment of flesh. By doing so He can say to you and me, no matter our emotional condition, temptations, or pain, "I understand."

He "dwelt among us, . . . full of grace and truth" (John 1:14). Jesus is full of grace. Because of His sacrifice, we don't get what we deserve, and that is called grace. And He is full of truth. It is only when His grace leads us to know the truth that we are truly free.

But that is not all. "We beheld His glory" (John 1:14). Paul said it like this: "Christ in you, the hope of glory" (Colossians 1:27). Have you personally beheld His glory *in you*?

Code Word: CONDESCENSION

When Jesus came and took on flesh, it was one of the most amazing acts of condescension to be found anywhere at any time. As you think of this code word today, marvel at how much you mean to Him.

Passion Proclamation

"I will not leave you comfortless: I will come to you."
—JOHN 14:18 KJV

Lord, You humbled Yourself in coming to earth so I could go to heaven. And one day, because of Your marvelous grace, I can go to where You are because You came to where I am. In Jesus' name, amen.

DAY 32

We had a really good start. Life began in a perfect paradise. The climate was never too warm and never too cold. We had no heartaches, no worries. We felt no aches or pains. We were doing wonderfully well—*until* we disobeyed and ate the forbidden fruit and were expelled from the garden.

The first evidence of this demise came when Adam and Eve saw "that they were naked" (Genesis 3:7). They had been naked all along, but not until sin came did they take their eyes off God and put them on themselves. This is always what sin does. Before, God had been the center of their attention and devotion. Sin entered the picture, and their focus became centered squarely upon themselves.

Their first impulse? Grab some fig leaves and cover their nakedness. But God in His grace intervened, because all the human mechanisms we use to try and cover our sin never suffice. He took an innocent little animal, killed it, and covered Adam and Eve with its skin. When that animal breathed its last breath, it became the first to know the expensive toll that sin takes on one's life.

God placed our first parents in a perfect paradise. We fell. God drove us out. And you and I have been trying to get back into His presence ever since. The account begins with paradise lost in Genesis and ends with paradise regained in Revelation. Right now we are exiles from Eden. But we are

making our way back home through the substitutionary sacrifice of Jesus Christ.

Code Word: SACRIFICE

"Without [the] shedding of blood there is no remission [of sin]" (Hebrews 9:22). Just as a sacrificial animal covered the sins of Adam and Eve, so the sacrifice of Christ on the cross is the only covering for our own sin.

Passion Proclamation

"The one who comes to Me I will by no means cast out."
—JOHN 6:37

Lord, I come to You now admitting I can do nothing in and of myself to cleanse my sin. I trust today in Your shed blood to cover me and cleanse me. Hosanna! Amen!

DAY 33

The Old Testament conceals Christ. The New Testament reveals Him! And there is no more vivid and visual foreshadowing of His substitutionary sacrifice for your sin than is found in the account of Abraham's sacrifice of his own son Isaac (Genesis 22:1–14).

God had promised Abraham he would be the father of a great nation. There was only one problem: he and his wife were old, beyond childbearing age, and his wife, Sarah, had spent a lifetime unable to conceive (see Genesis 17). And then they got their miracle: Isaac was born!

This was all too quickly followed by a time of testing: "Take now your son, your only son Isaac, whom you love . . . and offer him . . . as a burnt offering on one of the mountains of which I shall tell you" (Genesis 22:2).

Along the journey up Mount Moriah, the lad asked, "Father, where is the lamb for the sacrifice?" Abraham responded in faith, "The Lord will provide the lamb" (vv. 7–8, author's paraphrase).

In obedience to God, Abraham built the altar and placed his son upon it. And just at the right time, God was faithful to His word: "Then Abraham lifted his eyes and looked, and there behind him was a ram caught in a thicket by its horns. So Abraham went and took the ram, and offered it up for a burnt offering instead of his son. And Abraham called the name of the place, The-Lord-Will-Provide; as it is said to this day" (vv. 13–14).

Code Word: PHOTO

Today as you look at a picture on your desk or on your phone, let it be a reminder to you of this beautiful picture of Christ taking your place, dying your death, so you can live His life today!

Passion Proclamation

But without faith it is impossible to please Him, for he who comes to God must believe that He is, and that He is a rewarder of those who diligently seek Him.

—HEBREWS 11:6

Lord, what You promise You are faithful to provide. Like Abraham, I wait in faith, believing You to do "exceeding abundantly above all" I might ask or think.[3] In Jesus' name, amen.

We find another poignant picture of our coming Savior when we arrive at Exodus 12. One of the most important dates on the calendar of our Jewish friends is the evening they celebrate the Passover seder meal commemorating their freedom from death and deliverance from Egyptian bondage. God had sent a series of plagues on Egypt, where God's people were enslaved. The most devastating plague came on the night the death angel passed over every home in Egypt, bringing death to the firstborn of every family.

The Jews were instructed to take a little lamb—perfect and without blemish—slay it, and spread the blood over the doorposts of their homes so that when the death angel came, he would "see the blood" and "pass over" that particular residence (Exodus 12:13). The firstborn in those homes would be saved by the blood of the sacrificed lamb.

It is no wonder that fifteen hundred years later, when Jesus burst forth from the obscurity of the carpenter's shop and appeared in the Jordan Valley, John the Baptist pointed an index finger in His direction and shouted, "Behold! The Lamb of God who takes away the sin of the world!" (John 1:29). Would you, today, take a moment and behold the Lamb for yourself?

Code Word: FREEDOM

The sacrifice of the Lamb of God, the Lord Jesus, is what brings true freedom to your soul. Freedom is never free. It is always bought with blood. Rejoice today in the freedom Christ brings. God is not looking for human effort. He is looking to see if you have applied the blood of Christ to the door of your heart.

Passion Proclamation

The blood of Jesus Christ [God's] Son cleanses us from all sin.

—1 JOHN 1:7

"Dear dying Lamb, Your precious blood shall never lose its power, till all the ransomed church of God be saved, to sin no more."[4] *Hallelujah! Amen!*

Many of the recorded psalms of David point to the coming Messiah. There is a strong messianic appeal in his probing question in Psalm 24: "Who may ascend into the hill of the LORD? Or who may stand in His holy place?" (v. 3). Quick comes the answer: "He who has clean hands and a pure heart" (v. 4). That leaves me out, and I am pretty sure you as well.

My hands, representing my outward life, are not clean. And my inner life, my heart, is far from being pure. Like everyone's, my "heart is deceitful above all things, and desperately wicked" (Jeremiah 17:9).

How will we ever be able to ascend this hill, much less stand in God's holy place? There is only One who has walked this way and meets these two criteria: the Lord Jesus, the King of glory. His hands were clean and His heart was pure. Thus, knowing we were without hope, He came and His hands became dirty with the sin of the world, your sin and mine. And His pure heart became sin for us. Why? His clean hands became dirty so my dirty hands could become clean. His pure heart took my sin so my impure heart could become pure.

One day we will hear again the words from this psalm saying, "Lift up your heads, O you gates" (Psalm 24:7), and a multitude that no one can number will arrive with our King at the gate of heaven . . . and the King of glory will come

in, accompanied by everyone who looked to Him in faith for their eternal salvation.

Code Word: GATE

Today when you see or pass through a gate, let it remind you that the only way you will enter into the gate of heaven is through the Lord Jesus Christ. He is the door through which we enter.

Passion Proclamation

"Blessed are the pure in heart, for they shall see God."
—MATTHEW 5:8

Lord, I open wide the gate of my heart to You today. "Come in. . . . Come in today. Come in to stay. Come into my heart, Lord Jesus."[5] Amen.

Throughout the Old Testament we see foreshadows of the coming, promised Messiah. In the past few devotions, we have seen them in Genesis, Exodus, and the Psalms. As the sun of God's revelation to man continues to rise, we find it casting a perfect shadow when we arrive at Isaiah 53. This is, without question, one of the most vibrant pictures of our coming Lord to be found anywhere.

Isaiah, hundreds of years before Christ, framed it like this:

> He is despised and rejected by men, a Man of sorrows and acquainted with grief. And we hid, as it were, our faces from Him; He was despised, and we did not esteem Him.
>
> Surely He has borne our griefs and carried our sorrows; yet we esteemed Him stricken, smitten by God, and afflicted. But He was wounded for our transgressions, He was bruised for our iniquities; the chastisement for our peace was upon Him, and by His stripes we are healed. All we like sheep have gone astray; we have turned, every one, to his own way; and the LORD has laid on Him the iniquity of us all. (Isaiah 53:3–6)

He was wounded for our transgressions, though He never transgressed. He was bruised for our iniquities, though He never knew iniquity. And when we had all gone our own way, God took your sin, my sin, and "laid on Him the iniquity

of us all." He took your sin so you today can take on His righteousness.

CODE WORD: SHEEP

Sheep can't be trained. They are also directionless and defenseless, not prepared for flight or fight. That is you and me. Like sheep, we have gone our own way, but thankfully, the Lord laid on Christ the sins of us all.

PASSION PROCLAMATION

All we like sheep have gone astray; we have turned, every one, to his own way; and the LORD has laid on Him the iniquity of us all.

—ISAIAH 53:6

Lord, I don't always know the right way to go. I am so often defenseless. You are my Shepherd. Lead me today in the way You would have me go; I will follow. In Jesus' name, amen.

DAY 37

One of the most misquoted verses in all the Bible is found in Revelation when John, in his letter to the church at Ephesus, makes this accusation: "You have left your first love" (Revelation 2:4). Ask a hundred people who may have heard of this verse and the majority will remember it as saying, "You have lost your first love." But there is a world of difference in admitting that we left something and having to admit we lost something. The admission that "I left something" seems to carry more personal responsibility than simply saying, "I lost something."

Mary and Joseph could relate to leaving something. They had gone on an annual pilgrimage with twelve-year-old Jesus to Jerusalem and were returning home. Since Jesus was still a child, He could have traveled in the men's caravan or the women's. As Jesus' parents came to the end of the first day's journey, they realized He was not with either of them. It was not until they admitted they had not *lost* Him but *left* Him back in Jerusalem that they found Him—right there at the temple, in dialogue with the elders (Luke 2:42–49).

On your own journey to Jerusalem, could it be that you didn't "lose" your first love after all . . . you *left* Him? Go back to where you left Jesus, and you, like Mary and Joseph, will find Him right there.

Code Word: LEFT

If you are like me, most of the times when you think you lost something, the truth is, you left it somewhere. Let this be a reminder that we can never lose our love for Christ, although we may leave it from time to time.

Passion Proclamation

Be strong and of good courage, do not fear nor be afraid . . . for the LORD your God, He is the One who goes with you. He will not leave you nor forsake you.

—DEUTERONOMY 31:6

Lord, You are faithful. When I feel an estrangement, it is never because You have moved or left me. It is because I am the one who left my first love. Thank You for always being near. In Jesus' name, amen.

During His intense struggle on the cross, our Lord spoke seven times as He hung suspended between heaven and earth. The strangest of these cries was, "My God, My God, why have You forsaken Me?" (Matthew 27:46). He knew well what it was to be forsaken. In Galilee, He was forsaken by His family. They distanced themselves from Him, and we read that He had no honor "in his own house" (Matthew 13:57). In Gethsemane, He was forsaken by His friends when they ran away after He was taken by the mob (Mark 14:50). And at the end of the journey, at Golgotha, while bearing our sins, He was forsaken for a time by His Father so that we might never be forsaken.

Perhaps there is no more haunting word in our entire English language than the word *forsaken*. Many today know this reality. There are those who one day stood at a wedding altar, hearing the love of their life promise to "never leave or forsake" them. But they lied and left the gnawing pain of being forsaken. Countless children, abandoned by their fathers and/or mothers, also know the meaning of this cruel word.

Jesus truly knew its meaning. But He didn't give up. He reached up! This is a help and a hope for any of us who have been forsaken. He understands. Don't give up. Reach up.

Code Word: UP

So many times, when difficulties or heartbreak come knocking on our doors, we look at the swirling circumstances around us, or worse, focus all our attention on them. But look up. Be reminded that Jesus sees even the smallest sparrow that falls to the ground—and He cares so much more for you.

Passion Proclamation

When my father and my mother forsake me, then the LORD will take care of me.

—PSALM 27:10

Lord, I am so grateful that there is no fear of You ever forsaking me. I stand on Your promise that You will never leave or forsake me . . . never. In Jesus' name, amen.

DAY 39

That fateful night before the crucifixion, Jesus needed His friends and followers more than ever before. But on the heels of His agonizing prayer in Gethsemane's garden, He was seized by the mob. The Bible rather bluntly states, "All the disciples forsook Him and fled" (Matthew 26:56). All of them forsook Him in His greatest hour of need. But that is not all; they fled. They ran away into the darkness, some denying that they had ever known Him. And to make matters worse, this was not the action of His foes, but His friends.

There is a life lesson here for all of us. Instead of just giving in, Jesus made a choice. Hear Him under those ancient olive trees: "My soul is exceedingly sorrowful, even to death. . . . If it is possible, let this cup pass from Me; nevertheless, not as I will, but as You will" (Matthew 26:38–39). Our Lord reached all the way into the depths of His own being and chose to follow not His own will, but the will of the One who had sent Him.

We will all come to the place in our own experience where we must choose God's will over our own. Choose Him.

Code Word: MENU

Today, as you look at a breakfast, lunch, or dinner menu, let it remind you that life is filled with choices. Make sure

you choose God's will over your own. His way, His will, is always best.

Passion Proclamation

Choose for yourselves this day whom you will serve. . . . As for me and my house, we will serve the Lord.

—JOSHUA 24:15

Lord, today have Your will done in my life. Mold me. Make me according to Your will and not my own. In Jesus' name, amen.

One week after the bombing of Pearl Harbor, Franklin D. Roosevelt, in addressing the nation, said, "Those who have long enjoyed such privileges as we enjoy forget in time that men have died to win them."[6] Sadly, there is more truth than one might want to acknowledge in those words. In reading about Jesus' crucifixion, we are reminded of the words of our Lord: "Greater love has no one than this, than to lay down one's life for his friends" (John 15:13).

When you think about it, freedom is never really free. It is always bought with blood. Jesus never fought in a war or marched in step in an army. He simply trudged up and down the dusty roads of Judea and the hills of Galilee, meeting needs, giving hope and comfort, healing broken bodies and wounded lives. You would think He must have been loved for those acts of kindness. But He wasn't. Instead, He was despised and rejected. He carried His own cross to His place of execution, and there the blessed Son of God, the heaven-sent manifestation of love, extended His already-beaten body on a cross and died for you and for me.

As we meditate on this "greater love" today, allow me the liberty to paraphrase Roosevelt's words: "We who have long enjoyed the spiritual privileges we enjoy must not forget that the Lord Jesus died to win them."

Code Word: FRIEND

Today, as you talk, text, email, or have lunch with a friend, let it be a reminder to you of Christ's supreme sacrifice. Yes, "greater love has no one than this, than to lay down one's life for his friends."

Passion Proclamation

By this we know love, because He laid down His life for us.
—1 JOHN 3:16

Lord, You are the true Friend who "sticks closer than a brother."[7] May I never be counted among those who forget in time that You died for me. Amen.

W hen Dr. R. G. Lee, the late, great preacher, first went on a Holy Land pilgrimage, he, along with his tour group, came to Golgotha, the place of the crucifixion. Lee, moved with emotion, ran ahead of the crowd. When the others arrived at that sacred spot, they found him on his knees, with tears streaming down his cheeks. "Oh, Dr. Lee," one of them exclaimed, "I see you have been here before."

"No," he replied. Then quickly correcting himself, he said, "Yes, I have. Two thousand years ago." Then came the words of Galatians 2:20: "I have been crucified with Christ; it is no longer I who live, but Christ lives in me."

As our Lord hung on the cross, the crowd saw only one man on the center cross. But the Father saw not just Christ but you and me and all others who would put their faith in Christ. When we come to Jesus, God takes our old life from us ("I have been crucified with Christ") and puts a new life in us ("Christ lives in me"). The Christian life is not a changed life. It is an exchanged life. You give Christ your old life, and He puts it away in the sea of His forgetfulness. And He gives you a brand-new life, a new life in Christ. It is an awesome thought: "Christ lives in me."

CODE WORD: LOGO

We love to identify with things. Certain logos tell the world the brand of clothing we are wearing. We proudly show our school colors and logos. Look at your key ring. Most likely it bears the logo of your automobile. When you look at a logo today, let it remind you of the privilege you have to identify with Jesus Christ. Let others see Him through the "logo" of your life and lips today.

Passion Proclamation

I have been crucified with Christ; it is no longer I who live, but Christ lives in me; and the life which I now live in the flesh I live by faith in the Son of God, who loved me and gave Himself for me.

—GALATIANS 2:20

Lord, speak through my mouth today; look at others through my eyes; live through me today so those with whom I come in contact will see You in me for Your glory. In Jesus' name, amen.

It has been said that leadership can be characterized by certain punctuation marks. Some think leadership is characterized by the period, that is, the command: "Go here. Do this. Do that." Others say it is better characterized by the exclamation point, expressing enthusiasm, expectancy, optimism. But most often true leaders are characterized by the symbol that is bent in humility: the question mark. The Lord Jesus was always asking questions. In fact, the gospel accounts record more than one hundred questions escaping His lips. One day, at Caesarea Philippi, He got to the heart of His own exclusivity when He asked His disciples, "Who do *you* say that I am?" (Matthew 16:15). Today He asks us the same question. In fact, for each of us, this is the question of eternity.

When asking this question in the language of the New Testament, it is emphatic; that is, the "you" is placed for emphasis at the beginning of the sentence. It is as if Jesus were asking, "What about you? You and you only? Who do *you* say that I am?" God bless Simon Peter. We often bemoan his impulsiveness and quick temper. But here he came through: "You are *the* Christ, the Son of the living God" (Matthew 16:16). What do you say? This is a question you cannot avoid. Who do *you* say He is?

Code Word: TEMPERATURE

Today, when you check the temperature outside, let it remind you that scientific truth is narrow. Water freezes at 32 degrees Fahrenheit—not 33 or 34. That is narrow. How about math? 2 + 2 = 4 . . . not 3, not 7. So don't be surprised that theological truth is also narrow. Christ is the only way to eternal life. It is the very nature of truth: all truth is narrow.

Passion Proclamation

"I am the way, the truth, and the life. No one comes to the Father except through Me."

—JOHN 14:6

Lord, I believe that You are the one and only way to heaven, and I join Peter today in boldly acknowledging that You—and You alone—are the Christ, the Savior of the world. Amen.

Telling good news/bad news jokes was a part of growing up in our culture, like the pastor who stood up on Sunday to say, "The good news is we have enough money here this morning to pay off the church debt. But the bad news is, it is still in your pockets!"

When we come to Romans 6:23, we find some good news and some bad news. The bad news is "the wages of sin is death." We all find ourselves in this verse because the Bible says, "All have sinned and fall short of the glory of God" (Romans 3:23). A wage is what you get for doing something; it is something you have coming. Payday is coming someday. That is the bad news.

But the good news is this: "The gift of God is eternal life through Jesus Christ our Lord" (Romans 6:23b KJV). It is a gift . . . a free gift. It can't be earned, nor is it deserved. It is yours to receive by faith. Jesus dealt with the bad news two thousand years ago when He *became* sin for us on the cross (2 Corinthians 5:21). Yes, the wages of sin is death. Jesus paid this price so we can finish the verse with the good news that forgiveness of sin and eternal life can be ours right now by accepting this God-provided gift by faith.

CODE WORD: NEWSPAPER

Today, when you pick up a newspaper or read an article on-line, let it remind you that in the midst of all the bad news, the good news can be found in Christ. And the headline reads, "Jesus Saves!"

Passion Proclamation

As cold water to a weary soul, so is good news from a far country.

—PROVERBS 25:25

Lord, no one has ever given me a gift as expressive and expensive as Your gift to me in Christ; not just abundant life here and now, but eternal life with You forever! Unworthy as I am, I receive this gift of Christ. In Jesus' name, amen.

DAY 44

Along the journey to Jerusalem, Jesus came upon a colony of ten lepers isolated from everyone they knew and loved due to the contagious nature of their hideous disease. They shouted to Him for mercy as He passed by. He stopped, told them to go show themselves to the priests, and they were healed as they obeyed. They all were cleansed of their disease, but here the similarity ends.

Only "one of them . . . returned" (Luke 17:15) in thanksgiving. This leper, like the others, had a family to get back to, a business to tend to, but something was more pressing. We are not told his name. He belongs to that vast throng who live their beautiful lives and perform their selfless deeds in often anonymous ways. We may not know his name, but he is shouting to us today, "Get back to Jesus. Be grateful. Give thanks for all He has done for you."

Jesus looked at him and said, "Arise, go your way. Your faith has made you well" (Luke 17:19). Along your own journey to Jerusalem, remember that the God of this universe wants your thanks. And that is why the writer of Hebrews calls us to "continually offer the sacrifice of praise to God . . . , giving thanks to His name" (13:15).

CODE WORD: RETURN

Today, when you return home from the office or from some appointment, let it remind you of the importance of returning daily to Jesus to simply say thanks for the wonderful things He has done and is doing in and through you.

PASSION PROCLAMATION

Oh, give thanks to the LORD, for He is good! For His mercy endures forever.

—PSALM 107:1

Lord, it is good to give thanks to You and to declare Your loving-kindness in the morning and Your faithfulness every night. Thank You for the realization that You are alive in me right now. In Jesus' name, amen.

DAY 45

Given the situation you may be facing with the seemingly inadequate resources at your disposal, you may be prone to ask what Andrew asked on a grassy, green hillside along the journey to Jerusalem: "What are they among so many?" (John 6:9). Throngs of people had gathered in Galilee to listen to Jesus, and hunger had set in. A small boy was found who had a sack lunch of a couple of fish and five barley loaves. Most of us know the story. Jesus multiplied the loaves and fishes, had the disciples feed thousands of people, and then had them take up the leftovers.

He was just a little lad with a little lunch. Maybe you feel as Andrew did that day, comparing the *little* you have with the *big* challenge in your life. But little always becomes much when you factor Christ into the equation of your life.

That boy left home that morning with the potential to feed thousands of people and didn't even know it! I wonder, *Is the same true with you?* You have incredible potential wrapped up in you to bless so many people today, and you may not even know it!

The boy in this story gave all, and that exchange tapped the eternal resources of heaven and brought them down into the bankrupt affairs of men. And Jesus is still at it today.

Code Word: LUNCH

Today as you eat lunch, let it remind you that God looks upon you not for who you are right now but for who you could be. Like the lad with the lunch, you are a person of huge potential.

Passion Proclamation

For I know the thoughts that I think toward you, says the LORD, thoughts of peace and not of evil, to give you a future and a hope.

—JEREMIAH 29:11

Lord, help me see myself as You see me today: as a person of promise, a person of potential to be used for Your good and Your glory. Take my life. Use me, Lord. In Jesus' name, amen.

Comfort zones . . . we all have them, and many of us never venture out from them. There are certain social, political, religious, and even economic comfort zones from which many of us seldom stray.

Jesus told the story of a Samaritan, a member of a race despised by the Jews of His day, who came upon a fellow traveler along his way. The traveler had been beaten, robbed, and left bleeding on the side of the road. Some religious types had passed earlier and walked on by on the other side of the road, snuggled in their ecclesiastical garments and congratulating themselves for having never stooped so low as to attack an innocent traveler. But the Samaritan felt compassion, stopped, applied first aid, took the wounded man to an inn for extended care, and paid the bill (Luke 10:30–37).

Consider today the fact that you were that wounded one. Jesus saw you beaten by sin and lying on the side of the road. Overwhelmed by compassion and love for you, He left His own comfort zone of heaven, came into your world, clothed Himself in human flesh, and reached out to touch you. But that is not all! Like the Samaritan, He took you to a place of refuge, deposited you in His church, and promised that when He came back He would settle all accounts.

CODE WORD: POLITICS

When you read or hear of the politics of today, think about this: Do you just stay in your own comfort zones in life, only connecting with others who think like you and act like you? One of the things we learn as we follow Jesus is that comfort zones become obsolete when love enters the picture.

PASSION PROCLAMATION

I can do all things through Christ who strengthens me.
—PHILIPPIANS 4:13

Lord, Your Word says that I can do all things through You. Lead me in some way today to follow You out of my own comfort zone in order to be a blessing. Because if it is great to get a blessing, it is much greater to be a blessing. In Jesus' name, amen.

Along the journey to His appointment with the cross in Jerusalem, Jesus often taught His followers spiritual truth in the form of parables, short allegorical stories designed to reveal deeper life lessons. The most familiar and often repeated of these is the parable of the prodigal son, mentioned in an earlier devotion. It tells of a boy who came to his father, demanded his inheritance in advance, left home, and wasted it all in the bright lights of the big city. He ended up broke and working in a pigpen, feeding swine. Finally, he "came to himself," got up, returned home, and was welcomed into the loving and forgiving arms of his father and received a new beginning (Luke 15:11–32). Henry Wadsworth Longfellow referred to this parable as the greatest short story ever written.

We may call it the parable of the prodigal son, but Jesus' intentions were never for the boy to take center stage in the story. It is not about him. It is all about the father. Jesus began the narrative by saying, "A certain man had two sons" (v. 11). Read that sentence again. Who is the subject of the sentence? The father. He is the one on center stage. This is a story about the dad.

Along the journey to Jerusalem, Jesus was giving us a picture of our heavenly Father's unconditional love for you and me. He is standing on center stage, waiting . . . right now . . . to receive you back with open arms.

Code Word: WELCOME

When you use or hear this word today, let it remind you that God the Father has not abdicated His throne and is waiting with open arms to immerse you in His unconditional love.

Passion Proclamation

Keep yourselves in the love of God, looking for the mercy of our Lord Jesus Christ unto eternal life.

—JUDE V. 21

Father, how great is Your unfailing love for me, so vast beyond all measure, that You should give Your only Son to make a wretch like me Your treasure. Thank You, Lord. Amen.

When reading the parable of the prodigal son (Luke 15:11–32), we first see the father with an open hand. He let the boy go. Here is a dad wise enough to know that the way to keep his kids was to let them go and the way to lose them was to hold them too tight. He could have guilted the kid ("Are you trying to break your mother's heart?") or played the comparison game ("Why can't you be like your older brother?"), but he didn't. We see him here with an open hand, saying, "I release you." He let him go, but he never gave up on him.

Like the father in this story, your loving, heavenly Father has an open hand toward you. You are not a puppet. You are a person, with the ability to make decisions in life. And so, He lets you go . . . because the love you can voluntarily return to Him is indescribably valuable to Him. He may let you go your own way, and you may remove yourself from the environment of that love, but He will never stop loving you and never give up on you. He knows the way to keep you is to open His hands and release you.

CODE WORD: WASH

Today, as you wash your hands or look at your hands, let it remind you that God holds you in His hands today. He will never give up on you.

Passion Proclamation

For I am persuaded that neither death nor life, nor angels nor principalities nor powers, nor things present nor things to come, nor height nor depth, nor any other created thing, shall be able to separate us from the love of God which is in Christ Jesus our Lord.

—ROMANS 8:38–39

Lord, immerse me in Your love right now in this moment of quiet. I sense Your presence and abide in Your love. I do love You, Lord. In Jesus' name, amen.

Most of us know the story well. The prodigal runs out of money and ends up with the menial task of feeding swine in a pigpen (not a very desirable job for a Jewish boy, I might add!). But he comes to himself and heads for home. Jesus said, "But when he was still a great way off, his father saw him and had compassion, and ran and fell on his neck and kissed him" (Luke 15:20). The boy came walking . . . but the father went running! His love that was tough enough to release his son was now tender enough to receive him. Look at their embrace . . . no crossed arms, pointed fingers, clenched fists; no cross-examination of "Where have you been?" or "Where is the money?" Just open arms. His open hands turn into open arms.

The Father is waiting for us with open arms. How grateful we can be that God does not deal with us "according to our sins" or mistakes or failures but according to His tender mercies (Psalm 103:10). Is it time for you to "come to yourself" and return home to Him? When you do, you will find Him with open arms, saying, "I receive you."

CODE WORD: OPEN

As you go through your day, opening doors, opening drawers, opening letters, let each act be a reminder to you that the Father has open arms for you . . . no pointed fingers . . . no crossed arms . . . just open arms of forgiveness and a welcome home.

PASSION PROCLAMATION

Love . . . does not seek its own, is not provoked, does not take into account a wrong suffered.

—1 CORINTHIANS 13:4–5 NASB

Lord, thank You for the blood of Jesus, which provides covering for my sin. "Amazing love . . . how can it be?"[8] In Jesus' name, amen.

I f you have ever memorized a verse of Scripture, most likely it is John 3:16: "For God so loved the world that He gave His only begotten Son, that whosoever believes in Him should not perish but have everlasting life." It is the verse most often heard in the simplicity and beauty of a little child's voice proudly reciting it from memory. And it is the verse most often whispered by aged saints as they breathe their last breaths. It is the entire gospel in a nutshell.

John 3:16 speaks of the *cause* of this great salvation: "For God so loved . . ." The single motivating factor behind God's entire redemptive plan is His love for you and me. This beloved verse also speaks of the *cost* of this salvation: "He gave His only Son." Jesus paid a high price to redeem us to Himself—death on a Roman cross outside the city gates of Jerusalem. And salvation's *condition*? "Whosoever believes in Him . . ." That speaks of me. It speaks of you. And any and all may come, placing their faith in Him alone. Finally, this verse speaks of salvation's *consequence*: we "should not perish but have everlasting life." Those without Christ are perishing . . . a little more each day.

Let God love you today as you meditate on this old and oft-repeated promise.

Code Word: GIFT

What do you do to get a gift? You don't earn it or deserve it. Someone who loves you very much gives it freely to you, and all you have to do is receive it. God's gift of eternal life, although purchased at great expense, is a free gift. Your part? Receive it by faith.

Passion Proclamation

The gift of God is eternal life in Jesus Christ our Lord.
—ROMANS 6:23

Lord, thank You for loving me even when I am so unloving. Your love has no boundaries. I receive Your unconditional love right now by faith. In Jesus' name, amen.

Arguably, no one else's dying words have been more quoted or more memorable than those of Jesus of Nazareth. Nailed fast to a Roman cross, He spoke seven times. After a long night filled with betrayal and false arrest, lying testimonies and illegal trials, cruel mockery and a bloody scourging, Jesus' hands and feet were nailed to a cross, and it was dropped with a *thud* into a hole in the ground.

It was nine o'clock in the morning, and He hung on that instrument of death until noon, when a strange and mysterious darkness covered the earth for three hours. Shortly thereafter, He died. But before we mourn His death, take to heart His gracious dying words.

Jesus' first words from the cross were a prayer: "Father, forgive them, for they do not know what they do" (Luke 23:34). Jesus died praying for others. What He preached about loving enemies to a crowd in Galilee (Luke 6:28), He practiced on a cross on Golgotha.

Next came a promise to a man hanging near Him: "Today you will be with Me in paradise" (Luke 23:43). It is never too late for a new beginning.

Then, seeing His mother in the crowd, He pronounced to John, "Behold your mother!" and to His mother, "Woman, behold your son!" (John 19:26–27). Jesus gave John the responsibility of caring for His mother because He Himself was no longer Mary's Son; He was now her Savior!

Code Word: HAMMER

The next time you pick up a hammer to repair something in your home, let it remind you that Christ died an agonizing death, nailed fast to a Roman cross . . . for you.

Passion Proclamation

"It is the Spirit who gives life; the flesh profits nothing. The words that I speak to you are spirit, and they are life."

—JOHN 6:63

Lord, help me today to see others through Your eyes, even those who have spoken against me, and help me love them with Your amazing and unconditional love. In Jesus' name, amen.

For three hours total darkness enveloped the earth as Jesus hung on the cross. Darkness in the middle of the day! From the darkness came the piercing cry of the most haunting of all the words of Christ from the cross: "My God, My God, why have You forsaken Me?" (Matthew 27:46). This question has perplexed the minds of believers for centuries. Did a loving Father forsake His only Son in His greatest moment of need?

Many of us know far too well from our personal experiences the raw heartbreak that comes when we are forsaken by someone we love. Does God forsake His own? Did He forsake Shadrach, Meshach, and Abed-Nego in a fiery furnace (Daniel 3) or Daniel in a lions' den (Daniel 6)? No! Then why this strange cry escaping the bleeding lips of our Lord?

The prophet Habakkuk reminds us that God the Father is so holy He cannot look upon sin (Habakkuk 1:13). In the words of Isaiah, "All we like sheep have gone astray; . . . and the LORD has laid on Him [Christ] the iniquity of us all" (Isaiah 53:6). On the cross Jesus took our iniquity, or sin, in His own body, suffering our shame, humiliation, agony, and death, all consequences we deserved. And for that period of time, the Father turned His face away, darkness enveloped the earth, and Jesus fought and won the battle of sin in our place. No wonder the Bible says, "Thanks be unto God for his unspeakable gift" (2 Corinthians 9:15 KJV).

Code Word: PRICE TAG

As you do your shopping, let every price tag you see remind you that your salvation, although a free gift, came at an expensive price: the blood of Jesus Christ, God's Son.

Passion Proclamation

[God] made [Jesus] who knew no sin to be sin for us, that we might become the righteousness of God in Him.

—2 CORINTHIANS 5:21

Lord, please give me a glimpse of Your holiness. You are holy . . . set apart. And my own sin is so serious it necessitated the cross. Forgive me, Lord. In Jesus' name, amen.

DAY 53

After the darkness two more words escaped Jesus' lips from the cross. The words heard by those around Him, now stunned by the mysterious and strange meteorological happenings of the day, were a request to meet His own physical need: "I thirst" (John 19:28). Here is a reminder of His own humanity. He was God, yes. But He was encased in a body of human flesh. He knew hunger, pain, thirst, emotions. He wept on occasion, and on others He laughed. Now, a simple plea. He was thirsty. But we should not fail to note that this cry of a personal need never came until after the battle of Calvary was fought and the darkness had turned back to light.

The next words came in rapid succession: "It is finished!" (John 19:30). The Greek word for "finished" here means that the debt is paid in full . . . your sin debt . . . mine . . . paid up, in full! Finished. Over. Done. Some seem to think that Jesus went to the cross and made a little down payment for our sin, and we have to work and earn our way the rest of the way home. No, never. He paid your sin debt in full. So much is behind that declaration, "It is finished!"

The last words from the cross were, "Father, 'into Your hands I commit My spirit'" (Luke 23:46). And then He died!

Code Word: BILL

The next time you receive a bill for your mortgage, utilities, or credit card, let it be a reminder that you will never get a bill from Jesus. He paid off your account in full. Every sin for which you once owed is stamped with these words: PAID IN FULL!

Passion Proclamation

You were not redeemed with corruptible things, like silver or gold, from your aimless conduct received by tradition from your fathers, but with the precious blood of Christ, as of a lamb without blemish and without spot.

—1 PETER 1:18–19

Lord, I am learning it is all about grace, Your marvelous, matchless grace. A simple thank-You seems so inadequate. Take my life and make it useful to You. In Jesus' name, amen.

The consensus of sociology confirms that the number one quest in life for most men and women is a search for a meaningful relationship. Many have never known even one. The younger generations are the products of a massive divorce rate in our culture, and many of them are homesick for a home they have never known. Truly meaningful relationships are few and far between. Thus, many young adults are on a search . . . desirous of just one meaningful relationship to enjoy.

Paul reminds us that "in Him [Christ] we have redemption through His blood, the forgiveness of sins, according to the riches of His grace" (Ephesians 1:7). Note those first two words: "in Him." What Christ has to offer is not a religion or a ritual but a vibrant and meaningful relationship in Him.

There are only three types of relationships in life: outward (your relationships with others), inward (your relationship with yourself), and upward (your relationship with God through Jesus Christ). And the bottom line? We will never be properly related to others until we are properly related to ourselves, and this will never happen until we discover how valuable we are to God and come into a relationship with Him by placing our trust in Christ alone.

Code Word: MIRROR

When you look at yourself in the mirror today, let it be a reminder to you of the three types of relationships and the fact that you will never find true self-worth until you begin with a personal relationship with Christ.

Passion Proclamation

But as many as received Him, to them He gave the right to become children of God, to those who believe in His name.

—JOHN 1:12

Lord, help me see clearly today that I will never be properly related to others until I am properly related to You. In Jesus' name, amen.

My wife, Susie, and I are fortunate enough to own a home and a car. Some time ago we had to replace some eaves along the roof line, not because the roof was leaking, but because we noted some rot in the wood. Periodically we take our car in for an inspection even though it is running smoothly. We call it "preventive maintenance." Most of what goes wrong with my house or car does so because of one word—*neglect*. Neglect has adverse effects on physical things, but it is much more dangerous in the spiritual realm.

The writer of Hebrews asked a probing question—"How shall we escape if we neglect so great a salvation?" (2:3). Along the journey to Jerusalem, there are three responses people give to the gospel. Some accept it. Some reject it. But most simply neglect it.

While many do not accept by faith the claims of Christ, most do not flat-out reject them either. Perhaps you, or someone you know, are among that vast throng of people who simply neglect Christ's continual call, deceived into thinking there will always be adequate time to name Jesus as Lord and Savior. The reality is, you will either accept Him or reject Him, for not to decide is to decide!

Code Word: CHOICE

As you go through this day, you are faced with one choice after another . . . where to eat lunch, what to order, and so on. Let each decision be a reminder that the greatest choice we can ever make is accepting Jesus Christ as our personal Lord and Savior. If you have not done that, what are you waiting for?

Passion Proclamation

I have set before you life and death, the blessing and the curse. So choose life in order that you may live.
—DEUTERONOMY 30:19 NASB

Lord, thank You for giving me the free will to make choices in life. I am not a puppet. I am a person in Your image. Help me choose Your will and Your way this day. In Jesus' name, amen.

I t is impossible to imagine the pain, the grief, the sorrow Christ endured in dying such a slow, agonizing death. The writer of Hebrews reminds us that it was "for the joy that was set before Him" that Jesus "endured the cross, despising the shame" (12:2).

Shame is a dreadful emotion. Our Lord was stripped naked . . . *naked* . . . before all the onlookers. He was then beaten like a common criminal and finally nailed to a cross. He endured the physical shame, the emotional shame, and what was worse, the spiritual shame as the Father turned away His face from all the vile sinfulness Jesus was bearing in His own body on the cross. Jesus, the heaven-sent Messenger of love, the beloved and only begotten Son of the Father, had to suffer not only the guilt but the shame of the sin of the entire world . . . murderers, molesters, racists, and oppressors of the poor.

Nine hundred years ago, an isolated monk, Bernard of Clairvaux, framed it best:

O sacred Head, now wounded,
With grief and shame weighed down.
Now scornfully surrounded, with thorns, thine only
crown. . . .
How art thou pale with anguish, with sore abuse and
scorn!

How does thy visage languish, which once was bright as morn![9]

Go to the cross today. Stay there for a while. Jesus' death deserves our serious reflection.

CODE WORD: PAIN

Today let every ache, every pain, be a reminder of how much more Jesus suffered, enduring the cross and "despising the shame" . . . for you.

PASSION PROCLAMATION

"I gave My back to those who struck Me, and My cheeks to those who plucked out the beard; I did not hide My face from shame and spitting."

—ISAIAH 50:6

Lord, saying thank You for the cross seems so inadequate. I seek to understand what Your death means to me. Your love is unfathomable, and Your mercy has no end. In Jesus' name, amen.

DAY 57

Have you noticed how a particular smell can bring instant memory recall of a particular place or a particular person from the past? It can be a powerful reminder of an event decades after it happened. One of my high school teachers wore a fragrance called Jungle Gardenia. It had a distinctive smell that would linger in a room long after she had left it. To this day when I get a whiff of it, my mind immediately races back to her.

Fragrance takes center stage in the story of Mary of Bethany. Along with her siblings, Martha and Lazarus, she was a devoted follower of Jesus of Nazareth. On one occasion Jesus, along with other invited guests, joined them in their home for a dinner party. After dinner Mary did an astonishing thing: she brought some very expensive and precious oil and poured it out on Jesus' feet. While some rebuked her for not selling it and giving the money to the poor, Jesus blessed her for this extravagant act of worship. Then John, who was sitting at the table with them, recorded, "The [whole] house was filled with the fragrance of the oil" (John 12:3).

Mary's gift became a blessing to everyone in the home that night who got caught up in its sweet fragrance. A life fully devoted to the Lord will have a lingering effect of His own sweet fragrance.

Code Word: FRAGRANCE

Today, when you inhale a certain fragrance, let it be a reminder to you of the importance of leaving behind the fragrance of Jesus wherever you go, "a sweet-smelling aroma, . . . well pleasing to God" (Philippians 4:18).

Passion Proclamation

For we are to God the fragrance of Christ among those who are being saved and among those who are perishing.
—2 CORINTHIANS 2:15

Lord, may my conversation and conduct be such that when I walk away from others today, the sweet fragrance of Your presence will remain. In Jesus' name, amen.

Thursday was a busy day. The disciples were hastily gathering the food and supplies necessary for the seder meal, not to mention trying to secure a room for the dinner. All was in order when they gathered on Mount Zion that fateful evening. And then they got into an argument, right there at the table. About what? Who of them would be the greatest in the coming kingdom Jesus had promised! At this point the greatest among them became the servant of all of them. Jesus arose from the table, girded Himself with a towel, and knelt before each of them to wash their feet. Whose feet needed washing the most that night? Whose feet in a matter of hours would be nailed fast to a Roman cross? And His were the only feet that left that night unwashed.

At the end of the meal, they sang a hymn and retreated beneath the olive trees of Gethsemane's garden to pray. Judas came in the shadows, followed by a mob with torches, and planted the kiss of betrayal on Jesus' cheek. Jesus called him "friend" (Matthew 26:50). To be attacked by the enemy is one thing, but to be betrayed by one of your closest "friends" is quite another.

Before we are quick to point a finger of accusation at Judas, or Peter, or any of the others who betrayed Jesus that night . . . we must ask ourselves, "Lord, is it I?" (v. 22).

Code Word: RELATIONSHIPS

When you think about a good friend today or interact with a group of friends at lunch or dinner, let it remind you that you have a true Friend, the Lord Jesus, who always "sticks closer than a brother" (Proverbs 18:24). Faith is not about rituals or religion. It is about a relationship with Jesus.

Passion Proclamation

"No longer do I call you servants, for a servant does not know what his master is doing; but I have called you friends, for all things that I heard from My Father I have made known to you."

—JOHN 15:15

Lord, I am no better than Judas. I may not have betrayed You for thirty pieces of silver, but I am too often quick to turn from my loyalty to You. May Your goodness, like a fetter, bind my wandering heart to You this day. In Jesus' name, amen.

At some time or another, most of us have been caught in a "Freudian slip," an inadvertent mistake in speech revealing an unconscious thought of some kind. This is closely akin to the "double entendre," a particular way of saying something that has a double meaning.

Having stripped Jesus naked, beaten Him with a whip, and battered His head with a reed, His enemies began to mock and spit upon Him. Then a Roman soldier spewed out sarcastically, "Hail, King of the Jews!" (Mark 15:18). They even nailed a sign over His head, stating, "THIS IS JESUS THE KING OF THE JEWS" (Matthew 27:37). Meaning this as a cruel joke, these soldiers unwittingly never spoke or wrote greater truth. He was a King, all right, but His kingdom was not of this world. He came to rule over the human heart . . . not on some earthly throne.

A few hours later, the religious types added their ignorance to the barrage of double entendres around the cross: "He saved others; Himself He cannot save" (Matthew 27:42). Unknowingly, they blurted out for all posterity the substitutionary aspect of Jesus' death. He could not save Himself and save us at the same time.

And who of us can forget the thief hanging next to Him? "If You are the Christ, save Yourself." Then quickly he added, "And us!" (Luke 23:39). Jesus could not do both. He died so we might be saved.

Code Word: SOVEREIGN

Let these three sayings, embedded in the larger story of the cross, remind you today of God's sovereignty over the events leading up to the crucifixion. He was in total control. Marvel at this, because you are a part of this story too.

Passion Proclamation

For the LORD is the great God, and the great *King* above all gods.

—PSALM 95:3

Lord, thank You for bearing in my place not only the pain and suffering but also the mockery and ridicule that accompanied it. Reign today as Lord on the throne of my heart. In Your name I pray. Amen.

magine you can smell the freshness of the cool Middle Eastern sunrise on the third day. The women arrive at the tomb early only to find that it is empty! Then they are startled by an angelic being informing them the Lord is not there but that He is risen. Then the angel says, "Go, tell His disciples—*and Peter*—that He is going before you into Galilee" (Mark 16:7).

One might have expected the angel to say, "Go, tell the disciples—and Pilate," or Herod, or any of the others who played a part in Jesus' indictment. Or, "Go, tell the disciples—and John." After all, John was the lone disciple standing at the foot of the cross that Friday. But our Lord knew Peter's heart. He was the one who had so blatantly denied Christ in the hour of testing and was in dire need of a word of encouragement, a new beginning, a second chance. These two words make all the difference: "and Peter"!

Many of us are in need of a second chance. Perhaps you, too, have faced your own setbacks or sorrows. Perhaps you need these two little words today: "Go, tell the disciples—*and* [put your name here]." One failure doesn't make a flop. You can have a new start, a new life, a new beginning. The second chance is not only possible but profitable . . . as Peter found out.

Code Word: BASEBALL

One of the things each spring season brings is the sound of the cracking of the bat as baseball season begins. Let this be a reminder that even though you might strike out, you get to bat again! The gospel is the message of the second chance.

Passion Proclamation

But this I call to mind, and therefore I have hope: The steadfast love of the Lord never ceases; his mercies never come to an end; they are new every morning; great is your faithfulness.

—LAMENTATIONS 3:21–23 ESV

Lord, I thank You that no matter what I may have done . . . or not done, the blood of Jesus Christ cleanses me from all sin and provides for me a second chance. Your love never ceases, and Your mercies know no end. In Jesus' name, amen.

PART 3

GOD IN US

That good thing which was committed to you, keep by the Holy Spirit who dwells in us.
—2 TIMOTHY 1:14

Bethlehem (God *with* us) and Golgotha (God *for* us) would be incomplete without Pentecost (God *in* us). This great and awesome God who stepped out of heaven and clothed Himself in human flesh to be with us, who went to the cross to die for us, now lives in every one of us who have trusted in Him for our salvation—and with the promise that He will never leave or forsake us!

The apostle Paul, when inquiring of those early believers in Ephesus about their knowledge of the Holy Spirit, was met with this reply: "We have not so much as heard whether there is a Holy Spirit" (Acts 19:2). Sadly, the same response could be heard from many believers today. The emphasis on who the Spirit is—and what He does—is lacking in much of the modern church. So, in these next few pages, let us set out to meet the Holy Spirit.

In short, the Holy Spirit is God Himself. An invisible yet inseparable Person of the Trinity: the Father, the Son, and the Holy Spirit. Too often, He is the forgotten member of the Godhead. Much is made of the Father and the Son and not enough of the Spirit. The Holy Spirit is God coming to indwell us, never to leave us, and to empower us for Christian service. It is the Spirit who convicts us of our sin, draws us to Christ, seals our faith, and gives us power to live the Christian life.

If you have believed on Jesus Christ, then the Holy Spirit has come to take up residency in your life. He is alive *in you* right now!

Code Word: HOME

There is no place like home. And "home" for the Holy Spirit is in your heart. Today when you come home and get comfortable, remember that your heart is where the Spirit of God lives and makes His home.

Passion Proclamation

To them God willed to make known what are the riches of the glory of this mystery among the Gentiles: which is Christ in you, the hope of glory.

—COLOSSIANS 1:27

Lord, thank You for the realization, right this very moment, that You—through Your precious Holy Spirit—are alive in me today. Lead me and use me for Christ's own glory. In Jesus' name, amen.

Promises made are valuable, but promises kept are invaluable. On the eve of the crucifixion, Jesus made an amazing promise to His disciples and to us: "I will pray the Father, and He will give you another Helper, that He may abide with you forever—the Spirit of truth" (John 14:16–17).

The key to understanding the true identity of the Holy Spirit is wrapped up within the word *another* in this promise. There are two Greek words translated into our English word *another*. One, *heteros*, means another, but of a different kind. We get our word *heterosexual* from this word. The other word, *allos*, means another of the exact same kind. For example, if I showed you a fountain pen and then showed you another pen—a cheap plastic pen—it would mean "another," but of a different kind. However, if I showed you a black Mont Blanc pen and then another one identical to it, then it would mean "another" of the exact same kind.

The latter is the word Jesus used in describing this Helper to come. In essence, Jesus was saying, "I am leaving, but I am coming back to abide in you forever. The Holy Spirit is *Me*!" He is the same make and the same model. Jesus kept His promise, and His Spirit comes to live in us, with the added promises to never leave us and to empower us to serve Him.

Code Word: PROMISE

Many of us are pretty good at making promises and then, for one reason or another, forgetting them or just not keeping them. But this never happens with Jesus. When you think about the promises you have made, let them remind you that Jesus always keeps His promises to you.

Passion Proclamation

For the promise is to you and to your children, and to all who are afar off, as many as the Lord our God will call.

—ACTS 2:39

Lord, thank You for the wonderful fact that You don't just make promises; You keep them. Great is Your faithfulness to me. In Jesus' name, amen.

One of the most liberating discoveries in the life of the believer is awakening to the importance of the personality and the deity of the Holy Spirit. If He is your constant companion, living in you, it stands to reason that you want to know Him in the intimacy of a close and abiding personal relationship.

Many are on a quest to "get more" of the Holy Spirit. But He is a Person, not some mystical force or substance. If we know Christ, we have all the Holy Spirit we will ever need. When we begin to think of Him in terms of some external force that might enable us or empower us with various kinds of supernatural abilities, then our quest will lead us on a journey to seek more of Him—and that is a dead-end road.

But when we think of Him as He really is, a Person, then our search will not be in trying to *get more of Him*; rather, we will be consumed with how we might *give Him more of us*. The Holy Spirit is a Person. He lives in you. His desire is to get more of you. And this happens when you surrender every area of your life to Him.

Code Word: ROOM

Like me, you have several rooms in your heart: a family room, a professional room, a social room, and so forth. Christ's desire is to be Lord over all the rooms in your life.

Today, when you enter a room, let it remind you to search your own heart and give Him more of you!

Passion Proclamation

"He will give you . . . the Spirit of truth, whom the world cannot receive, because it neither sees Him nor knows Him; but you know Him, for He dwells with you and will be in you."

—JOHN 14:16–17

Lord, I have all of You I will ever need. The real question I must ask is, "Do You have all of me?" Search out my heart today and reveal those parts of me I have not yet given to You. In Jesus' name, amen.

Each person of the Godhead plays a vital role in our salvation. The Father is the *source* of salvation. It all stems from Him. From the moment Adam and Eve ate of the forbidden fruit, and God slew an innocent animal to clothe them with its skins, His plan of salvation through blood atonement kicked into gear—culminating, ultimately, on a Roman cross outside the city gates of Jerusalem.

If the Father is the source, then the Lord Jesus is the *course* of our salvation. The road to an eternity with the Father must come through Him who said, "I am the way, the truth, and the life. No one comes to the Father except through Me" (John 14:6).

The Holy Spirit is the *force* behind it all. When giving final instructions to the disciples, Jesus said, "If I depart, I will send Him [the Holy Spirit] to you. And when He has come, He will convict the world of sin . . . [and] will guide you into all truth" (John 16:7–13).

The word *convict* means to bring to light, to expose, to show one's fault. The Holy Spirit flips the switch, turning on the light and exposing our sin. Being thus convicted of our own sin, the Holy Spirit then draws us close to Christ and performs the work of regeneration, for the Bible says we are born again "of . . . the Spirit" (John 3:5, 8).

Code Word: LIGHT SWITCH

Today, when you turn the light on in a darkened room, let it remind you of the convicting power of the Holy Spirit in your own life, exposing your sin before your eyes. Then confess it and forsake it!

Passion Proclamation

"He [the Holy Spirit] will glorify Me, for He will take of what is Mine and declare it to you."

—JOHN 16:14

Lord, You are my Convictor, Converter, Comforter, and Completer. Without You, I would be hopeless and helpless. Fill me with Your power today. In Jesus' name, amen.

There is something within most of us that loves to identify with certain brands. We wear clothing that proudly displays particular logos. Our key rings proclaim the logos of the cars we drive. And who of us with deep loyalty to our colleges or universities does not proudly proclaim it through all types of logos on bumper stickers, hats, and shirts?

Did you know that the Holy Spirit has some unique logos of His own that describe who He is and what He does? For example, fire is an emblem of the Holy Spirit. Fire speaks of the Spirit's consuming power in the life of the believer. John the Baptist told his followers in the Jordan valley that Jesus would "baptize [them] with the Holy Spirit and fire" (Matthew 3:11).

While the dove is perhaps the most prominent logo describing the Holy Spirit, another is wind. Wind speaks of the incredible depth of His mighty power to regenerate us. Jesus said, "The wind blows where it wishes, and you hear the sound of it, but cannot tell where it comes from and where it goes. So is everyone who is born of the Spirit" (John 3:8).

We may not be able to see the wind, but we can certainly see its power blowing the leaves in the trees. So it is with the Spirit. We may not be able to see Him, but we can certainly see the powerful effect of His presence all around us.

Code Word: BRAND

Today, if you pick up a writing pen with its logo or put on a shirt with its brand, let it be a reminder that the Holy Spirit desires to imprint your very soul with His own presence and identity for all the world to see.

Passion Proclamation

"By this all will know that you are My disciples, if you have love for one another."

—JOHN 13:35

Lord, in the midst of my identifying with so many good things, help me never to be ashamed of identifying with the greatest One of all—You! In Jesus' name, amen.

Some believers today seem to be confusing two very important words in our Christian vocabulary—*influence* and *power*. We seem to pride ourselves on influence, particularly when it comes to the arena of politics. On every front, it seems we are seeking to influence those in high places. We picket and protest, pass resolutions and sign petitions. Some of us even have access to the highest offices of the land to express our grievances and our desires.

People in the early church faced plenty of challenges. Too often, they were trying to keep from being burned at the stake or thrown to wild animals in one of Caesar's venues. When you think about it, it makes our problems—like fighting Washington to keep our tax-exempt status intact—relatively mundane.

These early believers did not have enough *influence* with the authorities to keep Peter out of prison (Acts 12), but they had something better. They had access to the *power* of the Holy Spirit to pray him out . . . and they used it!

The Holy Spirit living in you has far more power to get things done than any influence you could ever hope to wield.

Code Word: INFLUENCE

The Bible says each of us has been assigned an "area of influence" (2 Corinthians 10:13 ESV). In the midst of wielding your influence for good, don't forget that you have unlimited power—through the Holy Spirit who is dwelling in you right now!

Passion Proclamation

"You shall receive power when the Holy Spirit has come upon you."

—ACTS 1:8

Lord, You said "all authority (all power)" is in You (Matthew 28:18 AMP). If all power, all authority is in You, and You have given Your authority to me (Luke 10:19), then Satan has none . . . except that which I yield to him and his deceit. Fill me with Your power today, so there is no room for the evil one. In Jesus' name, amen.

After the Resurrection, the band of believers huddled in the Upper Room in Jerusalem with explicit instructions from the Lord: "Wait for the Promise of the Father . . . 'you shall be baptized with the Holy Spirit'" (Acts 1:4–5).

Waiting is something many of us are not very good at. But waiting on the Lord is an essential element of Christian growth. Luke records Christ's final words to His followers immediately before "He was parted from them and carried up into heaven" (Luke 24:51). He said, "Behold I send the Promise of My Father upon you; but tarry in the city of Jerusalem until you are endued with power from on high" (v. 49).

When reading this in the original Greek text, we discover an amazing truth. The word *endued* is in the middle voice. That is to say, the subject is not acted upon by another but acts upon itself for its own benefit. What happened in the Upper Room before the Holy Spirit fell on the believers? Jesus' followers were getting themselves right with God and then getting right with each other. They were not passively sitting around waiting. They were taking action upon themselves. When we get right with God ourselves—and get right with others in the process—we, too, can expect God to manifest His awesome presence in our lives.

Code Word: WAIT

Today when you have to wait for a phone call, a table at a restaurant, or an appointment with your doctor, let it be a reminder of the importance of patience, of waiting for the promise of your Father.

Passion Proclamation

Wait on the LORD; be of good courage, and He shall strengthen your heart; wait, I say, upon the LORD!

—PSALM 27:14

Lord, help me see how moments of waiting are really a laboratory for learning the depth of Your rich truths. In Jesus' name, amen.

DAY 68

The streets of Jerusalem were jammed with the masses of Jews who had descended upon the city for the celebration of Pentecost, fifty days after the Passover. Jesus had ascended to heaven and, obedient to His instructions, the disciples had gathered in the Upper Room. On the day of Pentecost, suddenly there came into their room the sound of a mighty rushing wind followed by the sight of tongues of fire resting on each one's head. Then the disciples began to speak in languages and dialects they did not know, and people heard these utterances—each in his own language. Then the Bible records, "They were all filled with the Holy Spirit" (Acts 2:4).

This was a onetime event when the Holy Spirit came to dwell in every believer with the promise never to leave. Pentecost can never be repeated any more than Bethlehem or Calvary. Bethlehem was a onetime event when God came to be *with* us. Calvary was a onetime event when we see God *for* us on the cross. In like manner, Pentecost was a onetime event when we see God *in* us.

It is Pentecost that marks the time and place—the when and the where—that God first sent His Holy Spirit to indwell all His believers, to empower them (and us) for service great and small . . . with the promise never to leave us.

Code Word: BIRTH

Pentecost marks the birth of the church, those of us throughout the generations whom God has called out of the world to become a part of His body. As you celebrate the birthdays of family and friends, let it be a reminder that you and I are a part of something supernatural, the church of the Lord Jesus Christ.

Passion Proclamation

Do not be drunk with wine, . . . but be filled with the Spirit.
—EPHESIANS 5:18

Lord, thank You for the realization that, by being born again, You dwell in me this very moment by Your Spirit. Fill me with Your presence and power. In Jesus' name, amen.

s I have read and reread the Bible in preparation for the writing of these devotions on the Holy Spirit, I have been captured by the word *suddenly*. We find it here again on the day of Pentecost when the believers "were all with one accord in one place. And *suddenly* there came a sound from heaven" (Acts 2:1–2). What took place that day was not the result of some process of growth and development. No one was taught how to do what happened. It was not manifested by merit. It was the work of God, and it came *suddenly*. The disciples were surprised by God!

One of the problems with our modern, sophisticated church is that some of us have lost our expectancy, the wonder of it all in the work of it all. Remember the shepherds of Bethlehem? They were out tending their sheep, just like any other night, when *suddenly* a great angelic choir announced the Savior's birth (Luke 2:13). Paul was en route to Damascus when *suddenly* he saw a light from heaven (Acts 9:3). He and Silas were once in jail when *suddenly* a violent earthquake opened the prison doors (Acts 16:26).

Oh, the possibilities for us if we would only live in the realm of expecting the unexpected—the *suddenly*—today!

Code Word: SUDDENLY

The next time you are surprised by something or someone, let it be a reminder that more often than not, when we least expect it, *suddenly* we can be surprised by God Himself.

Passion Proclamation

"When He, the Spirit of truth, has come, He will guide you into all truth."

—JOHN 16:13

Lord, help me live today expecting the unexpected, for You still have a way of suddenly making the impossible possible. In Jesus' name, amen.

One of the many miracles that took place on the day of Pentecost was the believers speaking in other "tongues." Perhaps no other subject in Scripture has been as misunderstood as this phenomenon that took place when the Holy Spirit fell on that little band of early believers.

The Bible records that they "began to speak with other tongues, as the Spirit gave them utterance" (Acts 2:4). The Greek word for "tongue" here is *glossa*. We get our English word *glossary* from this word. It is linguistic. These were known languages. They were languages foreign to the speaker—ones he or she had never heard—but that they were supernaturally empowered to speak. The actual miracle was in the hearing. The Bible says, "Everyone heard them speak in his own language" (v. 6). The word for "language" here is *dialectos*, from which we get our word *dialect*.

So what happened? People were there from all over the world for Pentecost, and God performed a miracle. Everyone heard the message of the gospel not only in his own language but in his own dialect. And the result? Three thousand Jews became followers of the Messiah on that very day and scattered back across the Mediterranean world to their homes sharing this good news.

Code Word: MIRACLE

Some miracles may come your way that are huge, with no explanation but the intervention of God on your behalf. But most of our miracles come day by day and often "suddenly," when we may least expect them.

Passion Proclamation

Though I speak with the tongues of men and of angels, but have not love, I have become sounding brass or a clanging cymbal.

—1 CORINTHIANS 13:1

Lord, the greatest miracle of all is the new birth . . . the way You met me where I was, forgave me of my sin, came into my life by Your Spirit, and live in me, now and forever. In Jesus' name, amen.

DAY 71

On the day of Pentecost, not only were the believers "*all* with one accord in one place" (Acts 2:1), but they were "*all* filled with the Holy Spirit" (v. 4). Not some of them . . . all of them. They had been baptized into the body of Christ and sealed by the Holy Spirit, and now they were filled with all His fullness. While the baptism of the Holy Spirit is a once-and-for-all-time experience at conversion, the filling is to be repeated over and over in the Christian's experience. At conversion we have the Holy Spirit; when we are filled, He has us.

The Holy Spirit's work in our lives involves many factors. Among them is the baptism of the Holy Spirit found in 1 Corinthians 12:13: "For by one Spirit we are all baptized into one body." This brings about the indwelling of the Holy Spirit—"The Spirit of God dwells in you" (Romans 8:9). Then we are sealed with the Holy Spirit: "Having believed, you were sealed with the Holy Spirit" (Ephesians 1:13).

If you are a believer, God the Holy Spirit has come to live in you. And He is the guarantee, the seal, that secures your eternal destiny. No wonder Paul exclaimed, "Christ in you, the hope of glory" (Colossians 1:27).

Code Word: DOWN PAYMENT

A down payment is a good-faith gesture on our part that assures the ultimate completion of a transaction. The sealing of the Holy Spirit is God's down payment, the "guarantee of our inheritance until the redemption of the purchased possession, to the praise of His glory" (Ephesians 1:14).

Passion Proclamation

In Him you also trusted, after you heard the word of truth, the gospel of your salvation; in whom also, having believed, you were sealed with the Holy Spirit of promise.

—EPHESIANS 1:13

Lord, thank You for the realization that You are truly alive in me at this very moment and for the security of knowing I am "sealed" by Your Spirit, the guarantee of my inheritance in You. In Jesus' name, amen.

There is only one command in the Bible as it relates to the Holy Spirit. We are not commanded to be baptized in the Holy Spirit—if we have trusted in Christ, the Bible tells us we have already been baptized in Him. And we are not commanded to be sealed with the Holy Spirit, for this is God's own work in us. What we are commanded to do is found in Ephesians 5:18: "Do not be drunk with wine, in which is dissipation; but be filled with the Spirit."

Every verb has a number, tense, voice, and mood. When we parse this verb translated as "be filled," we discover that the number is plural. It is in the present tense, which indicates continuous action. The voice is passive, meaning that the subject doesn't act; it is acted upon by another. And the mood is imperative. That means this is not optional; it is a direct command. Putting all this together means that this verse is more correctly translated as, "All of us must always be being filled with the Holy Spirit."

God's desire is that instead of our trying to *get* more of Him, we might this very day *give* Him more of ourselves so that He might then fill us with His own Spirit and power.

Code Word: COMMAND

When you face issues in which you have no option, like paying your taxes or making a house payment, let it remind you that to be filled with all of God's presence and power is not an option but should be the daily, normal Christian life.

Passion Proclamation

For this reason I bow my knees to the Father of our Lord Jesus Christ, . . . that He would grant you, according to the riches of His glory, to . . . be filled with all the fullness of God.

—EPHESIANS 3:14–19

Lord, strengthen me by Your mighty power through Your Holy Spirit today. In Jesus' name, amen.

I awoke early this morning with the incredible realization that the Holy Spirit was alive *in me*. Think about that. And His desire is not to simply indwell us today but to fill us each moment of every day with His presence and power. Remember, God's only command regarding the Holy Spirit is this: "Be filled with the Spirit" (Ephesians 5:18). And how can you be filled, right this moment?

First, *confess* your sins to Him. Come clean. The Spirit doesn't fill dirty vessels. The Bible promises, "If we confess our sins, He is faithful and just to forgive us our sins and to cleanse us from all unrighteousness" (1 John 1:9).

Next, *crown* Jesus Lord of your life. Take yourself off the throne of your heart and put Him there. "For to this end Christ died and rose and lived again, that He might be Lord both of the dead and the living" (Romans 14:9).

Finally, *claim* this amazing truth by faith. Jesus said, "Whatever things you ask when you pray, believe that you receive them, and you will have them" (Mark 11:24).

What is more important: what God says or how you feel? Don't equate warm, fuzzy feelings with being filled by the Spirit—or the absence of those feelings with an absence of the Spirit. Instead, know that you are filled according to your faith. Go ahead . . . *confess*, *crown*, and *claim* the Spirit's filling by faith.

Code Word: GLASS

When you fill your glass with water or iced tea, or when you fill your cup with coffee, let it remind you that God's will for you is to "be filled with the Spirit."

Passion Proclamation

And the disciples were filled with joy and with the Holy Spirit.

—ACTS 13:52

Lord, I confess my sin to You, I crown You the Lord of my life, and I claim Your promises by faith. Fill me with joy and with the Holy Spirit. In Jesus' name, amen.

DAY 74

Anyone who has visited the Holy Land has likely been struck by the stark contrast of the two inland bodies of water in the state of Israel—the Sea of Galilee in the north and the Dead Sea in the south.

The Sea of Galilee is teeming with life, abundant with all types of thriving aquatic life. It is often crystal clear and a beautiful blue in color. The Jordan River's headwaters flow from a myriad of springs near Mount Hermon and journey south to where the river empties into the Sea of Galilee. From there, it finds its outlet at the southern end of the sea and continues its flow down the Jordan Valley until it empties into the Dead Sea.

The Dead Sea has earned its name for a reason. It is dead! No aquatic life whatsoever is found in its waters, and the sulfuric smell arising from it is nauseating.

What causes this difference between the two bodies of water? The Dead Sea only has an inlet. It takes in but does not give out. The Sea of Galilee, on the other hand, has both an inlet *and* an outlet. It not only receives; it gives away. So it is with the vibrant believer who not only receives God's fullness but also gives it away—and then, like the Sea of Galilee, is constantly being refilled with the Spirit.

CODE WORD: WATER

Whenever you see water today—whether it's in a sea, a lake, or a glass—let it remind you of these two very different bodies of water and of God's desire for you to be like the Sea of Galilee—receiving His fullness and giving it away.

PASSION PROCLAMATION

"Freely you have received, freely give."

—MATTHEW 10:8

Lord, make me simply a channel of Your blessing today. Fill me so that Your power flows through me to touch and encourage someone who needs hope this very day. In Jesus' name, amen.

During my boyhood days, my family would make an annual summer trek from Texas to the mountains of Tennessee to visit my great-uncle and -aunt. They owned a little one-room country store on the side of a mountain nine miles outside of Pikeville. I was a city boy and completely fascinated by life in the Tennessee hills without running water.

They had an old surface pump well outside the back door of their house. To use it, you would take a little water from a Mason jar and pour it into the pump to prime it. Then you would pump, pump, pump until the water started flowing. As long as you pumped, water would flow, but as soon as you stopped, so did the water.

There is another kind of well called an artesian well. It is dug deep until it hits an underground stream or river. You don't have to pump an artesian well. All you have to do is tap into it and the water flows and flows.

There are too many Christ followers like that old pump well. They are pretty shallow, and to get them to serve God, you have to prime the pump—and then pump, pump, pump. Then there are those who have tapped into the "river of life" and are being continuously filled with the Spirit. Their lives overflow with His fullness. Some want to be served, while those filled with His fullness want to serve. Which one are you?

Code Word: FAUCET

When you turn the water faucet on to wash your face, brush your teeth, or get a drink, let it remind you to tap into the living water of the Spirit's own fullness.

Passion Proclamation

"Whoever drinks of the water that I shall give him will never thirst. But the water that I shall give him will become in him a fountain of water springing up into everlasting life."

—JOHN 4:14

Lord, I am thirsty for You. Spring up, O well, within my soul, and make me a blessing today. In Jesus' name, amen.

Where is the evidence that we are being filled with the Spirit of the living God? Some say the proof is found in certain gifts of the Spirit that we may be supernaturally enabled to perform. Yet we can read even the lengthiest passage about the gifts—1 Corinthians 12–14—and not find a syllable, much less a verse, about gifts being an indicator of being filled with the Spirit. The gifts of the Spirit are not a sign of spiritual maturity. In fact, Paul wrote to these same Corinthian believers, saying he could not speak to them "as to spiritual people but as to carnal, as to babes in Christ" (1 Corinthians 3:1).

The more we know our Bible, the more we understand the importance of context. Thus, the proof of God's fullness in a life is found in the very context of His command for us to "be filled with the Spirit" (Ephesians 5:18). There is no period at the end of verse 18, but rather a comma, with the next three verses offering the evidence of God's fullness in our lives.

First, there is an *inward* evidence. We will have a song in our hearts as we sing and make melody in our hearts to the Lord (v. 19). Then there is the *upward* evidence of an attitude of gratitude, "giving thanks always . . . to God" (v. 20). Finally, there is the *outward* evidence found in the fact that we are "submitting to one another" (v. 21). These—not supernatural gifts—are the proof of the Spirit-filled life.

Code Word: PROOF

Today, when you need to prove a point about something, remember that the proof of God's Spirit filling you is seen in the song in your heart, your attitude of thanksgiving, and your submissive spirit to others.

Passion Proclamation

Let each esteem others better than himself.

—PHILIPPIANS 2:3

Lord, if You humbled Yourself and became a servant, how much more do I need to see others today as better than myself. Fill me with Your fullness, and help me to serve others today. In Jesus' name, amen.

The *inward* evidence that you are being filled with God's Spirit is "singing and making melody in your heart to the Lord" (Ephesians 5:19). This is what separates Christianity from other religions. Buddhists may have impressive temples, but they have no song in their hearts. Hindus may have their mantras and chants but no melody in their hearts. Islam may pride itself on its morality and mosques, but Muslims have no song in their hearts. When we are filled with God's Spirit, the first evidence is an inward joy, a song in our hearts.

Those of us who cannot carry a tune are thankful the instrument of this song is our heart and not our vocal chords! We may not be able to make much melody with our voices, but we certainly can with our hearts.

Note it is "melody" and not rhythm or harmony that is the evidence of the Spirit. Whichever of these three—melody, rhythm, or harmony—is dominant in a piece of music generally points to its intended appeal. Rhythm appeals to the flesh. Harmony appeals to the realm of our emotions. But melody? It appeals to the Spirit, that part of us that will live as long as God lives, which is forever.

You will know you are being filled with God's Spirit when you have a joyous song of melody welling up within you unto the Lord.

Code Word: SONG

Whenever you hear a song today—whether it's on the radio, in an elevator, or while you're waiting on hold—let it remind you of the inward evidence of God's Spirit working in your heart.

Passion Proclamation

Be filled with the Spirit, speaking to one another in psalms and hymns and spiritual songs, singing and making melody in your heart to the Lord.

—EPHESIANS 5:18–19

Lord, You are the melody in my life. Without You, there is no lasting joy. My heart sings praises to You this day. In Jesus' name, amen.

There is also an *upward* evidence of the Spirit filling our lives. "Giving thanks always for all things to God the Father in the name of our Lord Jesus Christ" (Ephesians 5:20). Note that our thanks is directed primarily "to God." When we realize that the Father is the source of everything and we allow His Spirit to fill us, our hearts will be full of thanksgiving "always" and "in all things."

I can hear those voices now: "But you don't know my problem." "But you don't know my husband." "But you don't know the situation I am in." You're right. I don't know. But God does, and this verse still says "always" and "for all things." Some of us only think of giving thanks when we get a blessing: we get a new job, we recover from an illness, or our wayward child comes home. But the evidence that God's own Spirit is filling us is that we give thanks "always for all things" even in the midst of our circumstances.

Remember Jonah? From inside the fish's belly, he said, "I will sacrifice to You with the voice of thanksgiving. . . . Salvation is of the LORD" (Jonah 2:9). And the very next verse says, "So the LORD spoke to the fish, and it vomited Jonah onto dry ground." Thanksgiving will set you free. It is the upward evidence of the filling of the Spirit.

Code Word: FISH

The next time you order fish for lunch or dinner, or see a fish in an aquarium, let it remind you that your situation is no worse than Jonah's . . . and that giving thanks has a liberating effect.

Passion Proclamation

In everything give thanks; for this is the will of God in Christ Jesus for you.

—1 THESSALONIANS 5:18

Lord, thank You, not necessarily for everything, but in the midst of everything. As I am filled with Your Spirit, fill me also with an attitude of thanksgiving, so that I might glorify You throughout this day and always. In Jesus' name, amen.

There is not only an inward and upward evidence to the filling of God's Spirit but an *outward* evidence as well. How will those who come into contact with us know that we are being controlled by God's Spirit? Paul framed it this way: by "submitting to one another in the fear of God" (Ephesians 5:21). That is, we are to live our lives esteeming other people as better than ourselves and putting them before us. It's not the things we say or the terminology we use that lets people know we are filled with God's Spirit; rather, it is how we act in our personal relationships with others that reveals the Spirit at work within us.

Christ is our example. See Him in the Upper Room, washing the disciples' feet. The greatest among them became the servant of them all. In a matter of hours, His own feet would be nailed to a Roman cross, yet He knelt before each of the Twelve to wash their feet. And yes, even the feet of the one who would so soon betray Him.

It is important to remember that this submission to one another is to be done "in the fear of the Lord." Living in the fear of the Lord is not a fear that God might put His hand *on* us in retribution, but a fear that He might take His hand of blessing and anointing *away* from us. We should live each day being careful not to say or do anything that might cause God to remove His hand of blessing from our lives.

Code Word: SINK

When you stand at the sink to wash your hands or brush your teeth, let it be a reminder of Christ washing the disciples' feet and for you to take on the Spirit of Christ, which is that of a servant to all, "submitting yourself one to another."

Passion Proclamation

"Whoever desires to become great among you, let him be your servant."

—MATTHEW 20:26

Lord, I am never more like You than when I am serving someone in a spirit of humility and submission. You must increase . . . I must decrease. Help me live out that truth today. In Jesus' name, amen.

Have you ever been thirsty? I mean, really thirsty? You might be inclined to spend two dollars for a bottle of water on a really hot day, but how much would you give for it if you were lost in the desert and dying of thirst? Money wouldn't matter. A truly thirsty person would pay any price.

Jesus said, "If anyone thirsts, let him come to Me and drink. He who believes in Me, as the Scripture has said, out of his heart will flow rivers of living water" (John 7:37–38).

The reason many of us are not being filled today is because we are not really *spiritually* thirsty. Thirst is a craving. Some of us thirst for worldly pleasures: cars, houses, "stuff" in all its shapes and sizes. Jesus reminded the Samaritan woman—and us—that whoever drinks of the things the world has to offer "will thirst again, but whoever drinks of the water that I shall give him will never thirst" (John 4:13–14).

We all know whether we are thirsty or not—thirst is painful. But if we have to ask ourselves if we are thirsty spiritually, then the chances are pretty great that we aren't. Do not settle for seeking to satisfy your thirst with the temporary things of this world; instead, seek the living water only Jesus provides.

Code Word: THIRST

Each time you feel that tinge of thirst welling up inside you, remember how necessary it is to be thirsty for the deeper things of God.

Passion Proclamation

Ho! Everyone who thirsts, come to the waters; and you who have no money, come, buy and eat.

—ISAIAH 55:1

Lord, as You invited, I come to You now and ask You to create a genuine thirst in me for the deeper things of Your Spirit. In Jesus' name, amen.

J esus' invitation to those of us who are thirsty is, "Let [them] come to Me and drink" (John 7:37). *Come* is one of the simplest words in our entire vocabulary. A little child understands the word and crawls to us to be picked up. Even our pets understand the word and rush to our sides. But in our more mature "wisdom," many of us hear Jesus' invitation to come to Him and seem to think He is saying, "Go." So we *go* and try to do more. We somehow think the busier we get with His work, the more we will please Him. When all along He is whispering, "Come to Me."

Come to Jesus, not to some new devotional program or some formula or even some spiritual gift. When we come to Jesus, we do with our hearts what little children learning to walk do with their feet. We simply come . . . to Jesus.

But that is not all we should do. It is not enough to thirst for Him or even to come to Him. His instructions are to "drink." Too many of us stop short. All the water in the world will not quench the thirst of a dying person unless he or she drinks! To drink of this water of life means to ask God to fill us with His Spirit.

Code Word: COME

Today, when your boss asks you to "come into the office," or your husband or wife says, "Come to the dinner table," let it remind you of Christ's invitation to come to Him at all times.

Passion Proclamation

"If anyone desires to come after Me, let him deny himself, and take up his cross daily, and follow Me."

—LUKE 9:23

Lord, I come to You. Take my will and my selfish pride and replace them with Your Spirit. I drink today of that fountain of life, and I hold fast to Your promise that I may never thirst again. In Jesus' name, amen.

DAY 82

In the midst of the Lord's invitation to us to come and drink, He inserted these words: "He who believes in Me, as the Scripture has said, out of his heart will flow rivers of living water" (John 7:38). God's blessings always turn on the hinge of faith. It is "he who believes in Me." Faith is the way we drink of this living water that satisfies our souls.

Jesus backed up this amazing promise by establishing a biblical basis for it from the Hebrew Bible: "as the Scripture has said." What Scripture? Jesus, no doubt, had in mind the words of the ancient prophet Isaiah: "The LORD will guide you continually . . . you shall be like a watered garden, and like a spring of water, whose waters do not fail" (Isaiah 58:11). Earlier the Lord had spoken to the Samaritan woman at the well, saying, "Whoever drinks of this water will thirst again, but whoever drinks of the water that I shall give him will never thirst. But the water that I shall give him will become in him a fountain of water springing up into everlasting life" (John 4:13–14).

The "living water" to which Jesus referred indicates that we are never to be stagnant; we are to be like a fountain or a river, always flowing to bless others. Drinking of the water that Christ gives is less about *getting* a blessing and more about *being* a blessing.

Code Word: DRINK

Today, when you take a drink from your coffee cup, water bottle, or other drink, let each intake awaken in you the invitation from Christ to come to Him and drink. And out of your heart "will flow rivers of living water" that will bless others (John 7:38).

Passion Proclamation

But he who doubts is condemned if he eats, because he does not eat from faith; for whatever is not from faith is sin.

—ROMANS 14:23

Lord, without faith You said it was impossible to please You. Not just hard to please You, but impossible! I do believe—and I pray that You would help me keep my faith firmly fixed on You. In Jesus' name, amen.

DAY 83

When we view the invitation to come to Jesus through the lens of the Greek text, it is passionately expressive: "If anyone thirsts, let him come to Me and drink" (John 7:37). The wording of the original text indicates this is a rather loud and deeply emotional outburst. Jesus was not speaking softly here. What amazes me is that we should even need this urging and that He should have to give it! Shouldn't it be the other way around? Shouldn't the tables be turned here? Shouldn't you and I be the ones pleading with Him to allow us to come? And yet it is Jesus who passionately pleads for us to come to Him!

I wonder who the thirsty ones are across the world right now. Some of us have tried so desperately to quench the thirst within our souls with the things this world offers—the new car, that certain someone, or any of a thousand other things. Yet it seems the more we have, the thirstier we become. Could it be that Jesus is opening your eyes to the reality that the something you think you need is really Someone?

Code Word: LOUD

Today, when you hear a loud voice or loud music, let it remind you that Jesus is standing before you, speaking with the most authoritative voice you have ever heard, looking at you with the most penetrating eyes you have ever seen, and pleading with you to come to Him.

Passion Proclamation

The Spirit and the bride say, "Come!" And let him who hears say, "Come!" And let him who thirsts come. Whoever desires, let him take the water of life freely.

—REVELATION 22:17

Lord, forgive me for thinking the things this world offers could ever truly satisfy. The something I have been searching for is really Someone . . . You. In Jesus' name, amen.

DAY 84

The fruit of the Spirit is love, joy, peace, longsuffering, kindness, goodness, faithfulness, gentleness, self-control" (Galatians 5:22–23). At first glance the sentence structure appears to possess a grammatical error—"The fruit of the Spirit *is* love, joy, peace" and so on. But the apostle is absolutely correct. This ninefold fruit of the Spirit is the outward evidence of the presence of the One living within us. The fruit of the Spirit is beyond our natural ability to produce, for it is inwrought and outworked by the Holy Spirit within us. It is He who is the Author of these attributes and the Source from which they flow. The fruit is *what we are*, and it is wrought in us by *whose we are*—not by anything *we do* in our own strength.

This fruit produced by the Spirit-controlled life manifests itself in three areas. First, when God's Spirit is ruling and reigning on the throne of your heart, it is expressed in your *countenance*—that is, your personal relationship with God, the expression of which is love, joy, and peace. Second, it is visible in your *conduct*, that is, in your relationship with others, the outward expression of which is longsuffering, kindness, and goodness. Finally, it is evidenced by your *character*—who you are in your relationship with yourself—the expression of which is faithfulness, gentleness, and self-control.

So, going forward, we must each ask ourselves this question: Is my life filled with the Spirit's fruit?

Code Word: GRAPE

Today, when you eat a grape from its cluster, or any piece of fruit, let it be a reminder to you that it was produced by the vine and did nothing in and of itself to present you with such a treat. The fruit of the Spirit produced in you is because of *whose* you are and not *what* you do.

Passion Proclamation

"Therefore by their fruits you will know them."
—MATTHEW 7:20

Lord, it is not anything I do that will bring honor to Your great name, but rather it is what You do through me. The fruit of the Spirit is love, so let Your love be shown through me. In Jesus' name, amen.

T he fruit of the Spirit is love, joy, peace . . ." (Galatians 5:22). The evidence of Spirit-filled living will not be in what we say or even in what we do. It will be written on our faces in our *countenance* of love, joy, and peace.

The first proof is found in *love*. The Greeks had three primary words that are each translated into our English vernacular as "love." One is a fleshly, sensual, or passionate kind of love. Another is a fondness or affection, a kind of brotherly love. And then there is God's love, *agape*. This is a selfless love that continuously seeks only the highest good for others—no matter what they may do to insult, injure, or humiliate us. *Agape* is the word Paul used here in Galatians 5:22. And it is certainly no coincidence that it appears first in this list of the Spirit's fruit. Why? Because all the other manifestations of the fruit are simply different expressions of this agape love.

In addition to love, *joy* will also be evident on the face of a Spirit-controlled believer. This is not the sort of joy that comes from defeating an opponent or escaping some trouble. Instead, it is a joy that only God can give, a joy that persists and endures even when the shadows of life come our way.

And then there is *peace*, that blessed inner tranquility that the Spirit-filled believer is able to draw upon when circumstances are anything but peaceful. It is the very peace Jesus promised when He said, "My peace I give to you; not as the world gives do I give to you" (John 14:27).

For the believer, love, joy, and peace join together to shine upon our faces—and give glorious proof of the presence of the One who lives within us.

Code Word: COUNTENANCE

When you look in the mirror, what do you see in your face? Love? Joy? Peace? Ask the Spirit to grow His fruit within you—so that it shines upon your countenance for all to see.

Passion Proclamation

The peace of God, which surpasses all understanding, will guard your hearts and minds through Christ Jesus.

—PHILIPPIANS 4:7

Lord, on my own, I can't love everyone, or be joyful in all things, or have peace in the midst of troubles. It is only through Your Spirit within me that I can be filled with Your love, Your joy, Your peace. Live through me to touch someone today. In Jesus' name, amen.

T he fruit of the Spirit is . . . longsuffering, kindness, good-ness . . ." (Galatians 5:22). When we live conscious of the Spirit's presence within us, we will have not only a counte-nance that reflects His presence but a conduct that reflects His character. This is expressed in our ability to be longsuf-fering, to offer kindness, and to exude goodness. And who of us does not need a little more of these things?

To be *longsuffering* is to possess patience. The word itself implies a refusal on our part to retaliate, even when we have been wronged. It is an extension of agape love—and love's greatest victory is often seen not in what it does but in what it refuses to do.

Kindness is an attitude we can clearly see in the life of Christ as He walked in this world. Simple but intentional acts of kindness go a long way in enabling others to see that Christ is alive in us. This kindness, sometimes translated "gentleness," has nothing to do with weakness. Rather, it is power on reserve and definitive proof that God's Spirit is influencing our lives.

And just as the Lord Jesus Himself "went about doing good" (Acts 10:38), we Spirit-filled believers will produce the fruit of goodness throughout our lives in our relationships with others. Our world is desperately looking for those who will offer patience, a little more kindness, and a lot more goodness. Won't you be one of them?

Code Word: STOPLIGHT

The next time you find yourself waiting at a stoplight, and the car in front of you doesn't go when the light changes to green, remember *Who* lives in you. Show some patience, a little kindness, and a lot more goodness to that driver—and to everyone in your day.

Passion Proclamation

Rest in the LORD, and wait patiently for Him.

—PSALM 37:7

Lord, I surrender anew to You so that when I come into contact with others today, they might see You—in me—demonstrated through longsuffering, kindness, and goodness. In Jesus' name, amen.

"T he fruit of the Spirit is . . . faithfulness, gentleness, self-control" (Galatians 5:22–23). These three offer the third proof of a Spirit-filled life. In our relationship with God, we possess a countenance that is obvious: love, joy, and peace. In our relationship with others, we display a conduct that is characterized by longsuffering, kindness, and goodness. But what about the relationship we have with ourselves? Our character should be one defined by obedience, which reveals itself in faithfulness, gentleness, and self-control.

Faithfulness here does not mean our belief in God. Rather, it has more to do with the faithful discharge of the duties entrusted to us. A large part of having an obedient character is steadfast dependability and consistency, dedication and commitment. When we are being led by God's Spirit, we become known for our faithfulness to all things good.

Gentleness implies a kind of strength on a leash. The word Paul used here describes an animal that has been domesticated, that has come under the control of its master. The word picture is of a wild stallion that has been broken. Once untamed, kicking and bucking, it is now controlled by the slightest move of the reins, turning left or right, stopping or going at the wish of its master. Only Christ living in us can tame our sinful nature and bring it under such control that we express gentleness in all our relationships.

The last of the Spirit's fruit is *self-control*. This is the ability to master our own passions, to literally hold them in

a firm hand. Self-control can never be fully realized on our own. It—like all the fruit—is only produced with the help of the Holy Spirit within us.

CODE WORD: PET

Today, when you give your pet instructions to come or to sit, and it responds in obedience, let it remind you that the Spirit living in you desires the same obedience from you.

PASSION PROCLAMATION

If we live in the Spirit, let us also walk in the Spirit.
—GALATIANS 5:25 KJV

Lord, true Christian character—which I so desire— only comes from the power of Your Spirit and can never be attained on my own. May my countenance, my conduct, and my character reveal Your presence in me to others today. In Jesus' name, amen.

DAY 88

Among my fondest childhood memories were the weekly Saturday morning football games on the old vacant lot. We began by choosing teams. There was one kid on my block that everyone wanted on their team. He was bigger and faster than the rest of us, and tougher to boot. When he was on your side, you knew you were on the winning team.

Are you aware that in the game of life, you have Someone very powerful on your side? That Someone is the Holy Spirit. The evening before the crucifixion, Jesus left His disciples—and us—with these words: "I will pray the Father, and He will give you another Helper, that He may abide with you forever" (John 14:16). And with the Spirit helping you, you can be sure that you are on the winning team.

The Greek word used here for *Helper* describes someone who is "called alongside" of you. This same word is translated "advocate" in 1 John 2:1. The word picture is of you being charged with a crime and taken before the judge. You stand there all alone. And then a person approaches the bench and speaks on your behalf before the judge, brilliantly pleading your case. You have just such an advocate on your side!

On that fateful evening Jesus was saying, "I am leaving you, but the Holy Spirit is coming to be on your side and by your side. He will never leave you."

Code Word: LAWYER

The next time you see a lawyer's office or come in contact with a lawyer, let it be a reminder to you that God, in the person of the Holy Spirit, is always by your side and on your side.

Passion Proclamation

And if anyone sins, we have an Advocate with the Father, Jesus Christ the righteous.

—1 JOHN 2:1

Lord, before anyone else, I choose You to be not just on my side but by my side . . . always and in all ways. In Jesus' name, amen.

Are you ready for an awesome thought to live with today? The Holy Spirit is alive and living *in you* right now! In fact, the Bible says, "Do you not know that your body is the temple of the Holy Spirit who is in you, whom you have from God, and you are not your own?" (1 Corinthians 6:19).

In the Old Testament, God had a temple for His people. There they would come to worship Him through the giving of their animal sacrifices. But in this new dispensation, God's temple is found in His people. You and me. We are His place of residence on this earth.

In the language of the New Testament, there are two Greek words we translate as "temple." One describes the entire temple area and the Temple Mount, including the area where Jesus drove out the money changers (Mark 11:15). The other describes the inner sanctuary itself, the Holy of Holies. This is the holy place where only the high priest—and he only once a year—could enter and commune with the *Shekinah* glory (the visible manifestation) of God Himself.

When Paul wrote of our body being the temple of the Holy Spirit, it was this latter word he used.

Think of it. You are God's Holy of Holies on earth. With such a Guest living in your heart, allow God to cleanse the temple of your heart today from anything and everything that might be unpleasing to Him.

Code Word: WORSHIP

Many of us are so body conscious. We trim and tone. Some of us even tuck! When thinking of your own body today, let it remind you that God is living *in you*, that you are His Holy of Holies—and take time to worship Him.

Passion Proclamation

For you were bought at a price; therefore glorify God in your body and in your spirit, which are God's.

—1 CORINTHIANS 6:20

Lord, to have paid such a high price for me, I must be of great value to You. Thank You for Your living presence in my life. Help me, each day, to more fully realize that You are truly alive in me. In Jesus' name, amen.

DAY 90

Have you ever had a confidential prayer partner? One you totally trusted and with whom you could confidentially share your deepest prayer needs? One who believed in you and with whom you agreed in prayer? Would you like to have a prayer partner like that? You already do! The Bible tells us, "The Spirit also helps in our weaknesses. For we do not know what we should pray for as we ought, but the Spirit Himself makes intercession for us. . . . He makes intercession for the saints according to the will of God" (Romans 8:26–27).

I don't know about you, but I often need help in prayer. I don't always know how I should pray about a matter. But the Holy Spirit in me does, and He always prays "according to the will of God." Yes, the Spirit can help you and me in our prayer lives. The word Paul used to describe how the Spirit helps us means literally to "lend a helping hand." The word picture is of two people carrying a log, one on either end, each dependent upon the other to hold up his end. The same Greek word appears in Luke 10:40, when Martha appeals to Jesus to get her sister, Mary, to help her in the kitchen with the preparation of dinner. In the same personal and practical way, we need the Holy Spirit to lend us a helping hand with our prayers—help we won't find in any earthly plan or program.

There is a powerful synergy at play when we recognize

we have a personal prayer partner in the Holy Spirit—One who is not just by our side and on our side, but alive inside us.

CODE WORD: DINNER

The next time you prepare dinner, set the table, or sit down to dinner, remember Martha—and the way she needed Mary's help in the kitchen is the same way you need the Holy Spirit's help in your prayer life.

PASSION PROCLAMATION

[One could] chase a thousand and two put ten thousand to flight.

—DEUTERONOMY 32:30

Lord, help me to know how to pray and what to pray and for whom to pray. I wait before You to listen to Your still small voice. In Jesus' name, amen.

We have a prayer partner, the Holy Spirit, who helps us in our "weaknesses" (Romans 8:26). And if you are like me, you are weak at times and need help with your prayer life. This should not come as a surprise. Do you remember the words of our Lord to His disciples in Gethsemane's prayer garden? "Could you not watch one hour?" (Mark 14:37). Jesus knew our weakness, so He sent us a prayer partner, the Holy Spirit, to help us.

The truth is we are no different from those men and women we read about in the New Testament. We "do not know what we should pray for as we ought" (Romans 8:26). Even the great apostle Paul unsuccessfully prayed three times regarding what he called a "thorn in the flesh." And then he heard from his prayer partner. The Holy Spirit whispered, "My grace is sufficient for you, for My strength is made perfect in weakness" (2 Corinthians 12:9).

The Holy Spirit lives in us to help us in our prayers, for we are all weak. We so often confuse our needs with our wants and do not know what is in our best interest. And there are times when we simply "do not know what we should pray." The something or someone we think we want is often not the something or someone we really need. But the Spirit knows exactly what we truly need—and He lovingly intercedes on our behalf with the Father.

Code Word: WANT

Today, when you see something you want, stop and ask yourself if it is something you really need. Many people run into heartaches in life because they get what they wanted, only to find out it was not what they really needed.

Passion Proclamation

And lest I should be exalted above measure by the abundance of the revelations, a thorn in the flesh was given to me. . . . I pleaded with the Lord three times that it might depart from me. And He said to me, "My grace is sufficient for you, for My strength is made perfect in weakness."
—2 CORINTHIANS 12:7–9

Lord, help me filter all my wants through the lens of what I truly need—those things that are for Your glory and my own good. In Jesus' name, amen.

We often speak of Paul writing the book of Romans, or John writing the Revelation, or Luke writing Acts. But the truth is, they, along with all the other Bible writers, were simply God's instruments through whom He gave us His Word. The Bible declares that "*all* scripture is *given* by inspiration of God" (2 Timothy 3:16).

Inspiration means the words are God's words, but He chose to deliver them through human channels. Peter shared the key that unlocks this mystery when he wrote, "Holy men of God spoke as they were moved by the Holy Spirit" (2 Peter 1:21). The Greek word translated "moved" is also found in the account of Paul's shipwreck, when he found himself in the midst of a violent storm accompanied by raging winds. Paul tells us that the sailors on board "could not head into the wind, we let her drive" (Acts 27:15).

Just as the sailors were active on board the ship, even though they had no control over where it went, so were the Bible writers. Though their personalities and styles are apparent, the writings were not their own. They were "moved" by the Holy Spirit to write what they wrote. The Bible you own was not given to you by those writers but by God Himself through the inspiration of the Holy Spirit. No wonder we call it the Word of God!

CODE WORD: BOAT

When you see a boat or an image of one, let it always remind you that "all scripture is given by inspiration of God." While the Bible writers were active in their writing, the words they wrote down were beyond their control. The Bible is God's inspired Word.

PASSION PROCLAMATION

Then the LORD put forth His hand and touched my mouth, and the LORD said to me: "Behold, I have put My words in your mouth."

—JEREMIAH 1:9

Lord, Your Word is a lamp unto my feet today and a light unto my path. Thank You for sending this love letter to me personally. In Jesus' name, amen.

We make much of the fact that Jesus forgives our sins. But did you know there is one sin that has no forgiveness? It is not murder or adultery or any of those other more blatant transgressions we are so skilled at pointing out in others. The Bible says, "Therefore I say to you, every sin and blasphemy will be forgiven men, but the blasphemy against the Spirit will not be forgiven men" (Matthew 12:31).

This unpardonable sin is not an act. It is not murder or adultery, and it is surely not something you might ignorantly say with your lips. The unpardonable sin is an attitude. Among the more memorable things Jesus said on His last evening on earth was, "When He, the Spirit of truth, has come, He will guide you into all truth" (John 16:13). To blaspheme the Holy Spirit is to reject His witness to your heart about who Jesus Christ really is—the Son of God. And if anyone reaches that point, his sin is unpardonable, and he is without hope.

This sin is not against the Father. Nor is it against the Son. It is against the Holy Spirit. It is not unpardonable because the Spirit is greater than the Father or the Son . . . but because His efforts come later! The Holy Spirit is God's final attempt to reach your soul with the message of salvation. No one is coming after Him. The Holy Spirit is God going as far as He can to save you without making you a puppet and overruling your will.

Code Word: CALLOUS

Look at that callus on your hand or foot. You can stick a pin in it and not feel it. A callus is to your hand what a calloused attitude is to your heart: hardened and unfeeling. We get our word *callous* from the same Greek word Paul used to describe those who become "past feeling" (Ephesians 4:19). It is not that God no longer calls us to Him but that we can no longer hear Him. So when you see that callus, remind yourself not to let your heart get calloused.

Passion Proclamation

Today, if you will hear His voice, do not harden your hearts.
—HEBREWS 3:15

Lord, my heart is open to hear Your voice right now. Speak, Lord—I wait before Your throne; Your promises I believe. And like Jacob of old, I will not let You go until Your blessing I receive. In Jesus' name, amen.

DAY 94

Did you know that when you become a believer, God stamps you with His seal of approval? The Bible says that when you put your trust in Christ, "you were sealed with the Holy Spirit" (Ephesians 1:13).

In the ancient world a seal was used to authenticate a document. A letter would be secured with hot wax and then *sealed* with the imprint of a signet ring to show it was real. The Holy Spirit is our seal to prove we are saved and secure: "The Spirit Himself bears witness with our spirit that we are children of God" (Romans 8:16).

A seal also shows ownership. Cowboys brand their cattle with hot irons to forever show others who the owner is. God seals us with His Spirit to let the world know we are His prized possessions and that we belong to Him, having been purchased at a great price.

The seal of the Holy Spirit also shows that we are secure—no one can snatch us away from God (John 10:28). The Roman soldiers sealed the tomb of Christ to secure His body and to prevent anyone from stealing it or tampering with it. Little did they know that their efforts to seal the *outside* of the tomb were useless against the power of the Lord *inside* the tomb! The same power that raised Jesus from the grave secures you in Him.

God has placed His own seal on you. It proves you are authentic, that you belong to Him, and that He will keep you secure forever.

Code Word: NOTARY

The next time you see a notary's seal proving a document's authenticity, let it be a reminder of the seal stamped on your own heart—the seal of the Holy Spirit.

Passion Proclamation

Do not grieve the Holy Spirit of God, by whom you were sealed for the day of redemption.

—EPHESIANS 4:30

Lord, may I live this day in such a way that it will be obvious to others that I bear Your brand, Your mark, Your seal on my heart. I want all the world to know that I belong to You. In Jesus' name, amen.

We are all familiar with bank deposits. The problem many of us face is making sure the deposits are enough to cover the expenses! Did you know that God has placed a deposit in you? The Bible says that God gives us the Holy Spirit, "who is a deposit guaranteeing our inheritance until the redemption of those who are God's possession" (Ephesians 1:14 NIV).

This deposit, or guarantee, is a promise of something more to come. Think of it this way: when you purchase a home, you put down a deposit—a down payment—showing good faith that you will complete the transaction. The Holy Spirit is God's down payment, placed in your life and stating to all that your final purchase is guaranteed.

The Holy Spirit in us assures us that the One who bought us with the price of His own blood is coming back. He is our "guarantee . . . *until* the redemption of the purchased possession" (Ephesians 1:14). If you put a $10,000 deposit down on a home, you are going to show up for the closing! Jesus paid a far greater price for you. And the Holy Spirit is His guarantee that He is going to return for you. Jesus will show up to close the deal.

Code Word: PAYCHECK

When you deposit your paycheck, let it remind you of the deposit God has placed in your heart . . . and the promise that eternal life is guaranteed to all those who believe and follow Him.

Passion Proclamation

In Him we have redemption through His blood, the forgiveness of sins, according to the riches of His grace.

—EPHESIANS 1:7

Lord, the joy of knowing You and loving You in the here and now is but a foretaste of what it will be in the then and there. I look forward to the day when You "close the deal" on the deposit You made in me. In Jesus' name, amen.

I wasn't a follower of Christ very long before a well-meaning friend asked me if I had been baptized in the Holy Spirit. Some believe this is a second work of grace after conversion, leading to a deeper life. Others attest to it being the second half of the first work of grace. But the biblical reality is that this baptism is not a baptism *of* the Holy Spirit but a baptism *by* the Holy Spirit into the body of Christ. The Bible says, "For by one Spirit we were all baptized into one body" (1 Corinthians 12:13).

The Holy Spirit is the baptizer who, upon our conversion, immerses us into the body of Christ. For thirty-three years the world looked upon the physical body of Christ. With His feet He walked among us, sometimes among great crowds and sometimes in the solitude of a single person. From His lips came the most tender and penetrating words ever spoken. Through His piercing eyes He looked straight into His people's hearts. Through His ears He listened intently to pleas for mercy. Through His hands He touched the points of greatest need.

Today you and I are the visible "body of Christ" being watched by a needy world so desperately in need of His touch. We each have a special place in His body—the church. And just as with our own bodies, when one part of the body suffers, it affects the entire body. You are vitally important to God, and His body will never be complete without you serving in the part to which you are assigned. There is something for you to do in Christ's body—something that no one else can do like you. Are you doing your part?

CODE WORD: DEPENDENT

Think today about how every single part of your body is there to perform a special function that no other part can perform. So it is in the body of Christ. Just as your hand needs your arm to function effectively, so we all are dependent upon each other in the body of Christ.

PASSION PROCLAMATION

For as many of you as were baptized into Christ have put on Christ.

—GALATIANS 3:27

Lord, what a privilege to be part of Your body, the church. Help me live in harmony with the other members so we might together present the world with a beautiful picture of You. In Jesus' name, amen.

The church, born on the day of Pentecost, is supernatural in its origin. It is also supernatural in its operation. "When He ascended on high, He . . . gave gifts to men" (Ephesians 4:8). Every believer (that includes you) has been given a spiritual gift "for the equipping of the saints for the work of ministry, for the edifying of the body of Christ" (v. 12). These gifts are given by God; they are not sought, caught, bought, or taught. In Romans 12, we find there are gifts of mercy, service, teaching, exhortation, giving, leadership, and the like. In 1 Corinthians 12, there are gifts of knowledge, faith, and various other supernatural strengths.

These sovereignly bestowed gifts are not rewards, nor are they natural abilities. They are supernatural gifts, given to every believer. No one has every gift, and no one gift is given to every believer. The gifts are distributed in God's perfect wisdom—and that is good! Because who of us would have gifted some rough, raw, callus-handed fishermen with the ability to preach, teach, heal, and bring thousands upon thousands to the foot of the cross in one generation?

You will learn to recognize your own gift—it's the thing you love to do, the thing that energizes you. For example, if mercy is your gift, you will find your greatest joy in reaching out to those in need. Your gift will also be publicly recognized. The body of Christ will use it—and God will be glorified by it.

Code Word: USE

The next time you use a gift someone has given you, remember the special and supernatural gift God has given you. Use it to build up the body of Christ all around you.

Passion Proclamation

To each one of us grace was given according to the measure of Christ's gift.

—EPHESIANS 4:7

Lord, all the natural ability in the world that I may possess will never compare to the power of the spiritual gift You have entrusted to me. Lead me to use it well. In Jesus' name, amen.

When you pray, are you aware that the entire Godhead—the Father, the Son, and the Holy Spirit—is at work? The Bible says, "For through Him [Christ] we both have access by one Spirit to the Father" (Ephesians 2:18).

The *source* of our prayer is the Father. All true prayer begins when we claim our relationship with Him: *our Father*. And the only way we can truly call Him Father is to be born again into His forever family. The Bible says, "As many as received Him, to them He gave the right to become children of God, to those who believe in His name" (John 1:12). We are all God's creation, but we are not God's children until we put our faith and trust in Him alone.

The *course* of our prayer is the Son. There is no access to the Father except through Jesus the Son, as the Bible plainly teaches, "There is one God and one Mediator between God and men, the Man Christ Jesus" (1 Timothy 2:5). Access to the Father in prayer is not through a priest or a church, or through anything or anyone apart from Jesus Christ. He is the only way to the Father's throne.

The *force* of our prayer is the Spirit. "The Spirit also helps in our weaknesses. For we do not know what we should pray for as we ought, but the Spirit Himself makes intercession for us . . . according to the will of God" (Romans 8:26–27). He is the force behind our prayers because He always prays according to God's will.

You may recite prayers without the Holy Spirit. You may

repeat phrases without the Holy Spirit. But you can never enter the Father's throne room of prayer unless you come through Jesus by the power of the Holy Spirit.

Code Word: TRAFFIC

The next time you use the GPS on your phone or your car to get you where you need to go, let it remind you that the only way to reach the Father in prayer is through His Son and by His Spirit.

Passion Proclamation

Now this is the confidence that we have in Him, that if we ask anything according to His will, He hears us. And if we know that He hears us, . . . we know that we have the petitions we have asked of Him.

—1 JOHN 5:14–15

Father, I come into Your presence only through the shed blood of Jesus Christ. Lead me to Your will for my life today through Your Word and by Your Spirit. In Jesus' name, amen.

Have you awakened to the reality that Christ is really alive *in you* in the person of His Holy Spirit at this very moment? The night before the crucifixion, Jesus said, "At that day you will know that I am in My Father, and you in Me, and I in you" (John 14:20). Today, fix your thoughts not on who you are, or what you are, or why you are, but on *where* you are.

Jesus revealed that He is positioned in the Father. Then, in the next breath, He said, "You [are] in Me"! No matter what may come your way today, you are in a good place. You are in Christ, and Christ is in the Father. Nothing can get to you that does not first have to pass through God the Father and God the Son to reach you. And if it penetrates that shield and gets that far, you can rest in the fact that there is a purpose for it in your life.

But that is not all. Jesus continued, "And I [am] in you." Can you see it? Christ is taking care of the outside of you (you are in Him), and He is also taking care of the inside of you (He is in you). What better place to live and have your being today!

Code Word: INSULATION

When you walk in your house and feel the warmth on a cold day or the cool on a hot day, that comfort is due, in large part, to the insulation you can't even see. Let that insulation remind you that, although you are not isolated from the world, you are insulated. You are in Christ, and He is in the Father—and in you.

Passion Proclamation

"Nevertheless I tell you the truth. It is to your advantage that I go away; for if I do not go away, the Helper will not come to you; but if I depart, I will send Him to you."

—JOHN 16:7

Lord, it is not who or what I am that matters to You . . . it is where I am: in You! In Jesus' name, amen.

The Bible is filled with invitations to come to God. Elijah of old challenged his hearers, pleading, "How long will you falter between two opinions? If the LORD is God, follow Him; but if Baal, follow him" (1 Kings 18:21). Joshua called the people of Israel to "choose for yourselves this day whom you will serve" (Joshua 24:15). Throughout the Old and New Testaments, bold voices continued to call men and women to faith in God.

The last invitation in all the Bible is found in Revelation 22:17: "The Spirit and the bride say, 'Come!' And let him who hears say, 'Come!' And let him who thirsts come. Whoever desires, let him take the water of life freely." Here we see not one, but two calls. There is an *outward* call: "The bride says come." The bride of Christ is the church. This outward call is given by the church in a myriad of ways through sermon and service. There is also an *inward* call: "The Spirit says come." This is the call of God Himself, knocking at the door of our hearts. We find this inward call in the experience of Lydia in the Bible when we read, "The Lord opened her heart to heed the things spoken by Paul" (Acts 16:14). Paul had given the outward call, but it was the Holy Spirit who issued the inward call to her heart, bringing about a transformation of life.

How can two people read a devotional book such as this, and one person experiences no real urging or need to come to Christ, while another person is drawn by supernatural power to a faith in Christ? One person may only hear the outward call, but the other also hears the inward call of the Spirit saying, "Come to Jesus."

"Today, if you will hear His voice, do not harden your [heart]" (Hebrews 3:15)—come to Jesus.

CODE WORD: RSVP

The next time you receive an invitation and are asked to RSVP, let it remind you of Jesus' invitation. He is saying to you, "Come," and the Spirit—in His still, small voice—is saying the same thing. Won't you come?

PASSION PROCLAMATION

For as many as are led by the Spirit of God, these are the sons of God.

—ROMANS 8:14

Lord, thank You for taking the initiative, for inviting me to come to You . . . before I ever thought of coming to You on my own. In Jesus' name, amen.

EPILOGUE

It may be that you have no problem believing that God is *with us*, that He came to Bethlehem and clothed Himself in human flesh and walked among us. You may even that God is *for us*, that He went to Calvary to die the death we deserved and to take our sin in His own body on the cross. But the question of eternity is this: Is God *in you*? Have you come to the place in your life—believing He came to be with you and died for you—where you have asked Him to forgive you of your sin? And have you transferred your faith and trust from your own human efforts to Him alone for eternal salvation?

It is impossible for the God of the universe to come and live in you without you knowing it. The Bible says the salvation experience is like going from death unto life (1 John 3:14), from darkness into light (1 Peter 2:9). Would it be possible to go from death unto life and not know it? Would it be possible to go from darkness into light and not know it? If there is the slightest doubt in your heart about whether Christ lives in you, you can settle it right now.

All other religions of this world center upon man trying to get to God through human effort, almsgiving, good works, or similar works. What makes Christianity different from all these others is that it is *not* the story of man trying to get to God; instead, it is the story of God coming to man. *God with us. God for us. God in us.*

Jesus said, "Behold, I stand at the door and knock. If anyone hears My voice and opens the door, I will come in to him" (Revelation 3:20). Picture, for just a moment, an imaginary door to your heart. Jesus, who came to be with us and died for us, is knocking on that door right now. If you would like to receive God's free offer of eternal life, you can respond now by opening the door and inviting Him into your life. And when you do, you can stand on His promise: "Whoever calls on the name of the Lord shall be saved" (Romans 10:13).

If this is the desire of your heart, you can pray the following prayer. Go ahead. In your heart, pray this:

Dear Lord Jesus,

I know I have sinned. I know I do not deserve eternal life. Please forgive my sin. Thank You for coming to be with me *and for taking my sin in Your own body on the cross and dying* for me. *My desire is for You to live* in me *now and forever. So I invite You now to be the Lord and King of my life. I turn to You, accepting Your gracious offer of forgiveness of sin and Your gift of eternal life. Thank You for coming into my life as my Savior and my Lord. Amen.*

A simple prayer can never save you, but Jesus can—and He will—if this prayer expresses the sincere desire of your heart. You can now claim the promise that Jesus left to all of us who would follow after Him: "Most assuredly, . . . he who believes in Me has everlasting life" (John 6:47).

Now you are ready to live the greatest of adventures—the one for which you were created in the first place—to know Christ and to walk with Him daily from this day forward. As you do, His Spirit, who now abides in you, will be at work to continue transforming you, making you more like Jesus in character and integrity.

MISSION:DIGNITY

All the author's royalties and any additional proceeds from the Code series (including *The Passion Code*) go to the support of Mission:Dignity, a ministry that enables thousands of retired ministers (and in most cases their widows) who are living near the poverty level to live out their days with dignity and security. Many of them spent their ministries in small churches that were unable to provide adequately for their retirement. They also lived in church-owned parsonages and had to vacate them upon their vocational retirement as well. Mission:Dignity tangibly shows these good and godly servants they are not forgotten and will be cared for in their declining years.

All the expenses for this ministry are paid for out of an endowment that has already been raised. Consequently, anyone who gives to Mission:Dignity can be assured that every cent of their gift goes straight to one of these precious saints in need.

Find out more by visiting www.guidestone.org and clicking on the Mission:Dignity icon, or call toll-free at 888-984-8433.

ABOUT THE AUTHOR

For more than twenty-five years, O. S. Hawkins served pastorates including the First Baptist Church in Fort Lauderdale, Florida, and the First Baptist Church in Dallas, Texas. A native of Fort Worth, he has three earned degrees (BBA, MDiv, and DMin), as well as several honorary degrees. He is president of GuideStone Financial Resources, which serves 250,000 pastors, church staff members, missionaries, doctors, nurses, university professors, and other workers in various Christian organizations with their retirement and benefit service needs. He is the author of more than forty books, including the bestselling *The Joshua Code*, *The Jesus Code*, and *The James Code*, and preaches regularly at conferences, universities, business groups, and churches across the nation. He and his wife, Susie, have two married daughters and six grandchildren.

Follow O. S. Hawkins on Twitter @oshawkins.
Visit www.oshawkins.com for free resources.

NOTES

1. William Newell, "At Cavalry," 1895.
2. James Weldon Johnson, *God's Trombones: Seven Negro Sermons in Verse* (New York: Penguin Classics, 2008), 15.
3. Ephesians 3:20.
4. William Cowper, "There Is a Fountain," 1772.
5. Harry D. Clarke, "Into My Heart," 1924.
6. Franklin D. Roosevelt, Proclamation 2524—Bill of Rights Day, November 27, 1941, American Presidency Project, http://www.presidency.ucsb.edu/ws/?pid=16046.
7. Proverbs 18:24.
8. Charles Wesley, "And Can It Be?" 1738.
9. Bernard of Clairvaux, "O Sacred Head, Now Wounded," 1153.

OPEN YOUR HEART TO

God's Word

The Joshua Code is designed to walk you through a year-long journey of meditating on one verse a week in order to recall and recite Scripture at will. Topics include temptation, understanding salvation, prayer, grace, vision, integrity, and more.

The Jesus Code asks one critical question each week to study and meditate on until the answer is firmly fixed in your mind and heart. Those answers will show God's will for your life, and they will help you feel confident as you share your faith with others.

One hundred percent of the author's royalties and proceeds go to support Mission:Dignity—a ministry providing support for impoverished retired pastors and missionaries.

AVAILABLE AT BOOKSTORES EVERYWHERE!

THOMAS NELSON
Since 1798

UNLOCK THE BLESSINGS IN

God's Word

The Believer's Code invites readers into a 365-day journey. Adapted from *The Joshua Code*, *The Jesus Code*, *The James Code*, and *The Daniel Code*, as well as brand-new applications and takeaways for readers, includes a short devotional reading, scripture, and a Code Word for each day, along with a challenge to put their faith in practice.

The Nehemiah Code—Who is not in need of a new beginning? Whether it be broken relationships, integrity missteps, or loss, most of us will spend some or much of the next year trying to restore something. The good news is . . . it's never too late for a new beginning.

One hundred percent of the author's royalties and proceeds go to support Mission:Dignity—a ministry providing support for impoverished retired pastors and missionaries.

THOMAS NELSON
Since 1798

PRAYER NOTES

PRAYER NOTES